The W... Of Wenatchee

A Collection of Natural Expression

Written by

The Breathers of Wenatchee Air

Edited & Curated by

C.G.Dahlin

Translators:

Anabel Watson

Dylan Eichenauer

Dalila Villamil

Contributing Writers:

Adam Leonardini (2)
Anabel Watson (5)
Barbara Ellen Baldwin (2)
Christine Ingram (2)
Claudia Yvette Zamorano (3)
Dalila Villamil (1)
Debra K. Rodgers (1)
Dylan Eichenauer (2)
Eric W. Fotherby (3)
Gloria Piper Roberson (6)
Gina Orlando (1)
Heather Kristoffersen (3)
Holly Crawford (1)
Jesemynn Cacka (5)
Jessica Mitchell (8)
Joan Crowe (1)
John E. DeHart (1)
Kacie Evans (2)
Katharine Kiendl (1)
Kevin Strickland (2)
Matthew Genther (2)
Maximus Ceballos (2)
Michael E. Bull (1)
Michael Reed Schooler (6)
Mike Morgan (4)
Mitch McCarrell (5)
L. Burton Brender (1)
Paiton Mabery (1)
Rachel Lynn Lippert (1)
Robert Cougar Penhaligon (1)
Susan Blair (2)
Sylvia B. (5)
Tyler Burlingame (3)
Ulises Navarro (1)

I.

II.

III.

IV.

V.

VI.

VII.

Editor's Note

This collection's creation was prompted by the notable creativity of the many people who pass through or call Wenatchee, Washington home. The Greater Wenatchee Area is what ties all of the contributing writers together. Their travels within and well beyond the valley all contribute to what substantiates what is being expressed within.

The themes and sentiments felt herein are what is carried in the hearts of the people that have breathed the air resting on the east side of the Cascades. The objective of this collection is to show the true soul and catharsis of those who have found themselves here, in one way or another.

With this considered, the undertone of this collection (poetry, short stories, and the unclassified in-between) shows what themes bring these diverse people together regardless of how their expressions and beliefs vary. This is what they naturally produce.

This collection was also assembled to counteract the conventions that modern publications typically take on, even in regards to standardized punctuation and format. None of the contributors paid a fee and there are no titled winners or honorable mentions. Those

who have been featured more than others have only
been so because of the sheer amount and diversity of
what they submitted. In this way, this project aspires
to be egalitarian in nature.

The writings you'll find herein were chosen for their
thematic-ness as opposed to some convoluted
concept of what is "good" writing or for the
contributors' submission to a predetermined theme.
Natural expression is the treasure of this work.

In other words, this collection aspires to be as
illustrative of the voices of this valley as possible. It
aims to show the authenticity and creativity of people
who've happened upon the Wenatchee Valley.

I

Sinking into the Ambiance

by Anabel Watson

Perhaps you'll close your eyes with me. Perhaps
you'll rest your mind, to let it flow free, safe and
softly, landing close to the ground amidst cushion
and quilt. Feel the warm security under a soft glow of
stringed orbs, auras of amber and gold. Notice these
orbs reflecting off earthy pots, hues of purple and
blue. Sink into this place. Relax. Ferns and vines
filling the pots, cleansed air that fills your core.
Beautiful, fresh and pure. Take a moment, a minute,
a breath - calm the mind and feed the soul.

Un Espíritu Indagador (Original)

by Dalila Villamil

Había una vez una niña llamada Curiosity. Ella vivía lejos de la ciudad, pero con las comodidades necesarias. Sus padres casi siempre estaban ocupados y dedicaban poco tiempo a su hija. Sin embargo, la pequeña Cury (como todos solían llamarla) se sentía muy amada con los cuidados y enseñanzas de su niñera Amaris.

El nacimiento de Curiosity fue muy interesante, pues ella concebido exactamente cuando el transbordador Curiosity fue lanzado al espacio el 26 de noviembre de 2011 a las 10:02 a.m., y aterrizó en Marte exitosamente el 6 de agosto de 2012, a las 05:31, hora en que Curiosity nació. Obviamente, un año después, los padres de Cury asociaron la hora de aterrizaje del transbordador espacial Curiosity con la hora de nacimiento de su hija.

Estas coincidencias encierran misterio en la vida de Cury y la hacen una niña especial. Por esta razón, los padres de Cury contrataron a Amaris, quien es una persona altamente capacitada, para instruir a su hija. A la edad de 2 años, Cury puede hablar fluidamente y es aficionada por temas espaciales.

An Inquiring Spirit (Translation)
by Dalila Villamil

There was once a girl called Curiosity. She lived far from the city, but with the necessary comforts. Her parents were almost always busy and spent little time with their daughter. However, little Cury (as everyone used to call her) was feeling very loved by the cares and teachings of Amaris, her babysitter.

Curiosity's birth was very interesting because she was conceived exactly when the Curiosity Space Shuttle was launched into space on November 26, 2011, at 10:01 a.m., and landed on Mars successfully on August 6, 2012, at 05:31, the date on which Curiosity was born. Obviously, a year later, Curry's parents associated the landing time of the Curiosity Space Shuttle with the birth time of their daughter.

These coincidences enclose mystery in Cury's life and make her a special girl. For this reason, Cury's parents hired Amaris, who is a highly qualified person, to instruct their daughter. At the age of 2, Cury speaks fluently and loves space themes.

A la edad de 5 años, Cury es extremadamente curiosa. Ella realmente disfruta preguntar sobre todo lo que se le ocurre. Y así, pasa el tiempo… Un día, caminando por el jardín, Cury cae en profundo sueño. Es el mejor sueño que alguien puede tener. "Niñita, acércate," dijo Dios. "Sí," dijo Cury. "Amas preguntar," dijo Dios. "Sí, tengo más preguntas que respuestas," dijo ella. Cury preguntó tanto como quiso.

No obstante, la pregunta que más llamó su atención dice así: "Dios, ¿qué haces para no aburrirte de vivir eternamente?" dijo ella. "Bueno, siempre estoy creando historias, y hago tantas que las estrellas no alcanzarán para enumerarlas", dijo Dios.

Cuando Cury despertó, escribió la respuesta de Dios en un poema. La estrofa central del poema es la siguiente:

Vida, aquí estoy
Quiero crear, crear, y crear
Como Dios crea
Sin cesar y enumerar

A partir de ese día, Cury sabe que su vida está destinada a crear, crear, y siempre crear.

At the age of 5 years, Cury is extremely curious. She really enjoys asking about everything that comes to mind. And so, time goes by... One day, walking through the garden, Cury falls into deep sleep. It is the best dream anyone can have. "Little girl come closer," said God. "Yes," Cury said. "You love to ask," said God. "Yes, I have more questions than answers," she said. Cury asked as much as she wanted to.

However, the question that most caught her attention was this, "God, what are you doing to not get bored of living eternally?" she said. "Well, I'm always creating stories and I make so many that stars are not enough to list them," said God.

When Cury woke up, she wrote God's answer in a poem. The central stanza of the poem is the following:

Life, I am here
I want to create, create, and create
As God creates
Without ceasing and numbering.

From that day, Cury knows her life is destined to create, create, and always create.

Coincidencia o no, el hecho es que las historias se conectan con propósitos que solo el tiempo revela. Este es el caso del transbordador Curiosity y el nacimiento de una niña que desarrolla el arte de indagar a través de las preguntas y quizás se convierta en un personaje revelador de conocimiento, arte y misterio. ¿Por qué no?

Coincidence or not, the fact is that stories connect with purposes that only time reveals. This is the case of the Curiosity Space Shuttle and the birth of a girl who develops the art of inquiring through questions and perhaps becomes a revealing character of knowledge, art, and mystery. Why not?

Untitled

by Jessica Mitchell

You know what's amazing? Having to choose between your psychological superpower and waking up and going to work every morning.

It's choosing between breakfast with your family and sleeping till noon because you missed another goddamn day of work again and again and again. My "abusive" absences, because you can't call in sad to work.

Today I have the superpower to be anything I want in my mind as long as I stay hidden beneath the covers of my bed. Hidden beneath the soft side of my lime green blanket because the other side's too scratchy thank you very much.

Four different prescription medications to get dressed and pretend that bipolar-depression-anxiety-OCD don't cloud my mind for every waking second. Hidden behind the drugs coursing through my brain.

Thoughts invade my mind. As I crash my car, lock the door, I worry yet again that maybe I really am the problem. I have slit my wrists so many goddamn times mentally. I have crashed and died. I have heard the scraping metal as the glass shatters and I scream. There are not enough tears to cover the racing images so I bite my lip until it bleeds.

I am not normal. I carry my mental illnesses like chains around my waist dragging me down and I just pray that you don't see them.

Stigma: because you can't call in sad to work.
Fear: but I'm only a danger to myself sweetheart.
Reality: is facing myself in the mirror. Accepting my limitations because if I can't why should you?

Away Song

by Gloria Piper Roberson

sunday evenings when they come to visit
they bring their backpacks and tech devices
even if I can't see it I feel it

we eat dinner their stomachs empty pits
vegetables cottage cheese and ham slices
sunday evenings when they come to visit

they put on cozy socks that I knitted
next year they'll have to be larger sizes
even if I can't see it I feel it

we play board games card games and read *widget*
beat drums shake tambourines and harmonize
sunday evenings when they come to visit

we have pillow fights we wouldn't miss it
they bring their backpacks and tech devices
even if I can't see it I feel it

they are nine years old - growing up a bit
my great grandsons my twins my prizes
sunday evenings when they come to visit
even if I can't see it I feel it

Homegrown

by Heather Kristoffersen

Mama said, "bless his heart," like that phrase could heal a man. And Daddy said, "be a man," like that was all it took. And I sat with idle hands and static lips, waiting for an excuse to keep my silence.

The clock hands quivered into place, and the bells chimed seven times. Dinner steamed on the table, poised on Mama's hand-knit potholders. The TV droned on about new things we ought to be afraid of, but it had become background noise. An all too familiar whirr of constant nagging, like the groan of a heater and the hum of a washing machine. It crept in subliminally until the whole world seemed something of a threat.

Daddy said, "That was a real good meal Mama." Like he was reading off some script sheet from an episode of a good old American TV show played on repeat, long after it should have been retired. And Mama said, "Well, a real good man bought me good ingredients." And this was their pledge of allegiance. And I could tell they never grew tired of it.

But I did.

12

Mama said, "Don't be hurt." And Daddy glared over the upturned bottom of his bottle as we listened to the glossy woman with the coy smile report another manslaughter over the clang of handcuffs. A house full of good country people stained the carpet red when the youngest boy had had enough. We looked to one another and in some ways we were all afraid.

Mama bit her tongue and Daddy said "Shut your mouth," to a table of already sealed lips. And we quaked in the stillness of the room. Our ears slaves to the drone of the static noise, blood draining from our heads to our toes, and flooding through our shoes until that dusty brown carpet seemed red.

xUnxLike (Father)

by Jesemynn Cacka

I am nothing like my father
except in the ways I'm a whore
marks of his women in forms of daughters
tallies of my men hatched by my middle fingers

I am nothing like my father
especially in the way I can swallow my pride
he would rather die alone than apologize

I am nothing like my father
except in the ways I am a liar
a sharp tongue to cut my heart
I oiled mine - soft and sated
with pain to hide the marks already formed
a sorted slight of hand

I am nothing like my father
especially in the way I love
unconditional don't-have-to-ask-twice love
I'll open up my heart and give you all I got

I am nothing like my father
except in the ways we are human

I am nothing like my father

except in the ways that I am

I am nothing like my father
except in the ways we are still trying to figure this
shit out

Statue

by Jessica Mitchell

I am nothing but what they've made me
standing naked in the roar of the crowd
twisting and gyrating as I slide down the pole
the smell of body butter and sweat is my existence
spreading my legs
baring my being
as dirty dollar bills are thrown to the floor

and later as I am pressed against the alley wall
he won't notice the hollows in my cheeks
my collarbone jutted out razor sharp
I am only the lackluster moans
as he pounds his flesh against mine

my body lies for me
as we go about this business
pseudo love
priced high enough to feed starving children
but I am starved
of touch
of meaning
but we are all starved of something in the end

and in the end
I am left dripping and empty
make up fixed upon my face

16

and the glitter covering my body
sparkles in the street lights

the illusion of happiness
purchased for a fee
I am what they've made of me
and I know not what else to be

Give Up

by Michael Reed Schooler

object the clear view

difficulty may your mentor be

sandstone young esophagus

make deaf the ears of god when they can hear you

laugh another day or more

on strains putting to listening

destitute and ardent prideful soul

the devil cheers you

isolate all visceral temptation

stare into the sun submerging

blindness finds the kindest guidance

harried forth escapading feet

correspondence met

successive blood-flow

contraction

and relief

The Waitress
by Barbara Ellen Baldwin

hated trying to tame
dishwasher blonde hair

hated sensible shoes
arch supports which didn't

hated absent supervisors
who had someone else
get up to sparkle windows

hated the very sun rising
a cartoon orb spiked yellow

hated every shrill wake up
morning another butt-dragging
eight hours ahead

hated her own breakfast
eggs bright always too bright

hated trying not to look
like she looked at work
washed out wanting to kick
something hated the local inn
a shriek of families
pouring through double doors

at four every afternoon
laughing like ninnies
wanting stuff she had to troop
back and forth fetching
food she

hated couldn't get
who would eat this
ask for something always or never
on the menu the menu she

hated fingerprints always
hers to clean torn rag
dragged over pictures
of pretend food every damn night

hated knowing the ones
laughing would think
of something not in print
she'd have to shuffle
off in tight shoes to ask
the chef about

hated his cheery retorts
whatever dish ordered
of course available

hated how he talked in big
letters loving unusual requests

she would have to carry
back to her tables later
wearing that look
the one she got
a facial tic forging
saying as little as possible
yes here are your basted eggs
of course we have them

certain the customer
made them up
the chef too
pulling a fast one
basted turkey maybe
but eggs beyond outrageous
meant to drive her right
over the edge

Daily Grind
by Sylvia B.

away I shall go
quiet I shall be
speak softly please
I have no time for distractions or meaningless
conversation
I don't want the drag of the day
I have been dragged
too far and too long
cut too deep to get road rash
mostly just bone now
all the bandages in the world wouldn't help me heal
this is a broken that cannot be fixed

Confused

by Maximus Ceballos

yeah I know my family wants to help

but I feel like I don't need help

cause all I feel like they're doing is giving me nothing

but mouth

and yeah I cry

makes me feel like I'm losing pride

but that doesn't mean shit

cause it feels like a kick to the ribs

all these emotions are rich

cause showing them makes me feel like a bitch

and it makes me start to itch

I get anxious and feel concerned

feelin like I have no one on my side

but maybe it's the drugs

making me feel all wack inside

it's putting me in denial

making me feel hella suicidal

why?

cause I feel fuckin fried

I feel unstable like a broken down table

and it sucks

cause it feels like I'm puking up my guts

and my family can see my cuts

I know they're sad and probably mad

but how the fuck am I supposed to get through this

without a dad

yeah maybe he was an ass

but that doesn't mean

I have to erase him from the past

so instead I just sip on my flask

but this life I'm living just feels like a game

and I keep getting played

over and over

but honestly fuck being sober

cause when I'm fucked up I feel numb all over

Untitled

by Tyler Burlingame

so tired in this dance

dazing down at the bend of a river

knowing I'll slide east and south

what else can I do but admire?

the direction or sustenance

I need in my open mouth and require

waiting to be found waking and sleepy

catching only subtleties

the future is a growing road

for you to decide if the way is right

apparently you'll have plenty of time

to

My Uncle Died Last Week

by Gloria Piper Roberson

My late father's youngest brother, Bob, blind and
crippled, died last week. He was my very last uncle.
We lifted his ashes to the Bugler's cry of Reveille:
Rise Soldier into the summer morning on the
mountainside of Cave Hill.

A jealous breeze bore his stories away. His medals of
bravery—Purple Heart, Bronze Star and Silver Star—
earned in Normandy, Belgium, France, and
Holland—that rest under his handkerchiefs in the
shallow, top drawer of his boyhood chest in his
bedroom. It will forever possess his windy shouts of
Geronimo.

Yet, for me there is no one left to say how much I
resemble my father.

II

Dust

by Heather Kristoffersen

the walls are painted black and white
with wood-framed family
ghosts trapped behind the dusty panes
among them it hangs
an imposter of something sweet
or at least a reminder
of something
that is not

it's barrel rust bitten
it's trigger gummed up
and arthritic
it almost looks at home
the hallway smells like
dried cod
cookies
and cologne
but when farfar tells the story
it's all gunpowder and tobacco

he was just a boy
raised familiar
with the snarl of a stomach
the breath of an enemy
and the stare of an empty man

his fingers
red as the patches plastered
to the uniforms of the men he cowered to
on the street

he walked
so only his footprints
in the fallen snow
remembered him once he passed

before him
the snow bloomed like roses
in norwegian spring
only it was winter and such vibrance
was no guest of the sun
nor beckoned by anything
so sweet

he saw a man
whose body was dusted with snow
and whose eyes were glazed over with ice
the man's uniform was stiffened with frost
and the gun
still holstered to his belt
was damp with blood
he took it and ran

just a boy
with a fascination and

surging adrenaline from
a drop of desperation

back home
with sunlight gushing in
like hot blood
I cannot feel
the chill of the white flakes
that once plastered his face

to me
that world vanishes as quickly as
his words fade to silence when
slippered feet
and withered
legs turn and tread
away

Dear Mother

by Gina Orlando

I feel your pain
I know you feel the weight of the world
and you want to make it better

we are your children
and it's hard to watch us suffer

I promise we are strong
and will do our best to right a wrong

we are in this together
please don't take all the blame

we love you no matter what
and will be together someday soon
near and far far away

Forged

by Jesemynn Cacka

forged by the fire we brace for every summer

flames always came in a rage

lives lost

homes burned forever

I've seen forests decimated

and the wildflowers that follow

nothing ever dies

it's only borrowed

burned down to make space for the new

birth - death - rebirth - repeat

primal woman

watch nature

follow suit

Fire Season

by Susan Blair

chinook blades beat the heated air

battering the calm

with their threatening thrum

they come not to harm though

but to aid in this

hotly contested strife

a breeze quakes the aspen

another whispers

the ponderosa pine

and my sodden body

cheers at this cooling

begging for more relief

these winds of my heaven

only send firefighters

farther into hell

Trails To Lakes

by Daniel Sconce

at the gentle beginning
the granite is worn to sand
ten thousand knobby soled shoes
shifting the weight of a weekend of life
anxious to have the trail ascend
wedged between an eon of stone
the backpacker's welcome-oracle
a forest service hand-carved the message
bold as the mountain itself
offers no alternative illustration
neither poetic distraction nor quaint alliteration
at this elevation where oxygen is rare
and trees foreshortened by gritty soil
the sign maker's intent is simplified
"TRAILS TO LAKES" is all it says
"TRAILS TO LAKES" nothing else implied
below the rough hewn letters
a meandering gouge from the carver's tool
climbs the weathered planks
unfolding the unseen switch-backs
stacked above and out of view
enticing the climber to shoulder his pack
follow each gold painted vein
to it's tethered balloon filled with blue
compare these jewels to a cloudless sky
the blue of dreams and the blue of eyes

trails to lakes are promises kept

each step a gain toward heaven's gate

a day of looking always up

of moving on and somehow knowing

the breeze will finally bring the smell of snow

a brief exhale from the seasons

tectonic plates and mountain ranges

holding ancient rain in deep stone basins

the trail turns and it is there

resting

reflective

cold and alone

where the finite finds the endless sky

an alpine gem ringed in stone

a piece of the sky returning home

What It Takes To Relocate In A State

By Eric W. Fotherby

The fawn-colored foothills recently dusted in an alabaster frosting of newly fallen snow rise up sharply, exposing the rock strata that proliferates these craggy cliffs with their unparalleled rugged beauty as they are gleaming in the morning sunlight, looming upwardly, rising majestically high up above from the shores of the mighty Columbia River.

Like a mighty wave sweeping forward in a westerly direction, the terrain flows through the earth's crust blending itself into the evergreen covered granite mountaintops to the West. White shining apexes that ascend in the backdrop of the setting sun create an eclipse between sun and mountain peaks that is darkening the early afternoon hours and blocking out the golden raiment that was meant for the inhabitants of the pass but who live in the shadows of the setting sun.

Meanwhile, dark conifers are intermittently obscuring and revealing the shining bright rays of the sun like a strobe light through the side window, flash-flickering on and off constantly in the driver's left peripheral view, blinding out that which is forward and in front of their vehicle.

The many travelers who routinely brave this route on an average daily and weekly basis for who knows how long and for who knows how many multiple times will know the risks and the hazards, but new dangers are always popping up, whether it be leaping deer or falling rocks.

Road Warriors that have made this treacherous journey on the ill-famed and infamous Highway US 2 while meeting giant semi-tractor trailer trucks on ancient undersized bridges at 60 miles an hour and flying around turns, spinning out gravel on the edges of cliffs without guardrails, makes this joyride a throat-gulping, panic-stricken, heart-stopping kaleidoscope of split seconds filled with trepidation and terror!

Throughout the total two hours and twenty minutes of white knuckled tension and acidic, constricted, stressed-out glands excreting excessive perspiration in temperatures of twenty-five degrees or less amidst a blizzard of snow in thirty mile an hour winter gales that create whiteouts that are less than thirty feet away from the front of one's truck and then it slides your vehicle halfway over into the oncoming lane before you can even have time to correct your internal gyroscopes motivateing one to keep extreme vigilance and alertness.

Avoiding oncoming traffic is the most serious concern for commuters with texters, alcoholics, and narcoleptics running loose, willy-nilly, all over the highways. When you see that oncoming car drifting over into your lane and you are literally trapped between a rock and a hard spot. That is an experience you will not forget!

It really requires a lot of determination in the first place to make the decision to pack up all of one's possessions and crossover from the dark side by the Puget Sound and to choose coming into the light. Physically loading and moving everything all of the way over the mountain pass and into Central Washington's sunny playground of extreme sports, wide open spaces and unlimited natural beauty.

This is a challenge, but not an insurmountable one. The return trip back home is the most pleasurable part of the journey, happily glissading in one's car back down the East Side of these gorgeous mountaintops, which are famously renowned as the Pacific Northwest Cascades. It really makes this part of the quest a wonderful cruise on a sunny day. In the end, the transmigration you will find is truly a wayfaring joy!

Genuine Intentions

by Anabel Watson

Let's go live in the forest. Let's build a home far from the sparkling cities of materialistic garbage - the falsified kindness - the hidden intentions. Let's journey where looks aren't deceiving, where, in fact, looks don't matter at all. Follow the stream and splash in a water sparkling so true to where a dip lies in the land. And pour into that dip a community of genuine intentions, where actions are read as they are, where the air is so pure it flows without a want for an identity or an opinion, where it observes and sees all to be true. Let's go there. Let's go there and never return.

Blessing

by Susan Blair

"It is morning, and I am the lucky one who is in it."
--- Mary Oliver

The scent of freshly mown grass anoints the recesses of my mind with the sacrament of this morning. I walk with the air teasing summer into fall. The leaves are trading their robes of green for priestly gold. A choir of starlings, singing every hymn they know, leads me to the beach and I follow, bent on benediction. As my feet churn the rocks, I sigh for grace: I am an elephant among angels. Widgeons dabble in a basin a few yards from the river's edge, wheezing their one-note whistle of thanks for the gift. Farther out, on a strip of sand between this pool and another, gulls huddle in silence before a heron rapt in contemplation. He has gathered his full height above them. Such reverence, such dignity! My eyes soar like a prayer to the foothills cloaked in vestments of sun and shadow. They promise absolution, redemption. I am embraced. Who is the sinner unblessed by this day? Nature is all the church I need.

Invernavera (Original)

By Claudia Yvette Zamorano

En marzo, la primavera se acerca a este hemisferio del planeta. Nunca he entendido esta división de hemisferios. No es que no la entienda, es que no me cabe. No la quiero entender y no hay más.

En marzo y la primavera se cuelan las alergias que se fueron en septiembre y visitan las narices de nuevo. Creo que a mí me está entrando la primavera por la garganta. Llevo semanas con una tos que comenzó muy sequita y me dejaba hablar con una voz mucho más grave y sensual (un bello disfraz para mi aguda voz).

Mira que era sequita, pero la primavera es húmeda y le dio por empapar al invierno que habita dentro de mí y comenzó a sacarlo a gargajos. Me hace un cosquilleo entre las cuerdas vocales, me ahoga, para que yo abra la boca y comience a toser y sacar el invierno. Mi invierno ha sido más resistente que la primavera.

Mira que ha sido muy maliciosa. Me ha hecho creer que yo ya era primaveral. Al echar vistazo adentro, pude comprobar que aún estoy con los tendones y los ligamentos sin hojas; aún no florece nada y en los pulmones me está nevando.

Winterspring (Translation)

by Claudia Yvette Zamorano

In March, spring approaches this hemisphere of the planet. I have never understood this division of hemispheres. It is not that I do not understand it, it is that it does not fit me. I do not want to understand it and that is all there is to it.

With March and spring sneak in allergies that left in September and visit noses again. I think that spring is coming down my throat. I have been coughing for weeks, a cough which started very dry and left me speaking with a much more serious and sensual voice (a beautiful disguise for my sharp voice).

Understand, it was dry, but spring is wet and began soaking the winter that lives inside me and began to expel it in the form of phlegm. It tingles between my vocal cords, choking me, so I open my mouth and start to cough and relinquish winter. My winter has been tougher than spring.

See that it has been very malicious. I was led to believe that I was spring. Upon taking a look inside, I could see that my tendons and ligaments are still without leaves; nothing yet blooms and it is snowing in my lungs.

Cosquilleo infernal en la garganta. Me están rallando las cuerdas vocales - hago pausa para toser. Comienzo a creer que todo esto ha sido culpa mía.

He llevado un suéter con flores impresas durante todo el invierno, ¿acaso habré logrado confundir a mi cuerpo? Quizás nunca sea primavera, quizás asociaba las flores con el frío del invierno y ahora solo exista inviernavera.

-Pausa para toser-

Acabo de toser. Confieso negarme a poner mis manos frente a mi boca y en ellas desechar los gérmenes. Siempre termino por estirar mi camisa hacia delante y toser ahí en el hueco que hay entre mi pecho y la ropa. Podría ser que inicie un ciclo en mi pecho: Primavera ha entrado por mi boca y los oídos, vaya se me ha metido hasta por los ojos, invadiendo la laringe y la trompa de Eustaquio. Está ahí dentro de mi tórax, ayudando al invierno a encontrar la salida por la faringe. Invierno ha sido expulsado; el sistema nervioso le da un aviso en cuestión de milésimas de segundos a mi brazo; mi brazo extiende a mi mano- mi mano hace un puño - utilizando únicamente el dedo medio y el índice, y estos dos crean un hueco que separa mi ropa de mi pecho. Mi cabeza se agacha impulsivamente. Acercando mi boca a ese hueco -

My throat tickles hellishly. My vocal cords are scratching - I pause to cough. I begin to believe that this has all been my fault.

I have worn a sweater with printed flowers throughout the winter, have I managed to confuse my body? It may never be spring, perhaps I associated the flowers with the cold of winter and now there is only winterspring.

[Pause to cough]

I just finished coughing. I confess I failed to put my hands in front of my mouth and in them discard the germs. I always end up stretching my shirt forward and coughing there in the gap between my chest and clothes. It could be that I start a cycle in my chest: Spring has entered through my mouth and my ears, it has gotten into my eyes invading the larynx and the eustachian tube. It is there inside my thorax, helping winter to find the exit through the pharynx. Winter has been expelled; the nervous system gives an alert in a matter of a thousandth of a second to my arm; my arm extends to my hand - my hand makes a fist - using only the middle finger and forefinger, and these two create a gap that separates my clothes from my chest. My head droops impulsively, bringing my mouth closer to that hole -

una lemniscata que parece olvidar que existen el verano y el otoño - y es ahí donde escupo en mi propio pecho al invierno. El invierno llega a la superficie de mi tórax en forma de un líquido secretado por las glándulas salivales en la boca, atraviesa la epidermis, la dermis, la hipodermis, para invadir este objeto al que he llamado cuerpo. Lo ves, esto es culpa mía y nunca podré salir de ese preámbulo. La aurícula, el canal auditivo externo, la membrana timpánica, el martillo Incus, el estribo, la cóclea, el vestíbulo del oído, el meato externo, las amígdalas, la región craneal, el diafragma, el esternón, las vísceras, el hipogastrio, la región lumbar, los glúteos, el sacra, el ilion, el isquion, el pubis, el hígado, el húmero, la tibia, el peroné, el yugular y aquellas zonas anatómicas que desconozco jamás podrán florecer a consecuencia de no querer arrojar el virus invernal hacia mis manos - tan sencillo sería plasmarlo en mis extremidades y pasar al lavabo a desecharlo - jamás podrán florecer sus jardines.

Aún cabe otra posibilidad. Quizás primavera me está presionando el cuello con una mano desde dentro. Quizás sean dos manos. Quizás hizo mancuerna con invierno. Quizás la segunda mano que siento es de invierno; por eso siento que se me va el aire. Por eso siento que me estoy muriendo.

a lemniscate that seems to forget that summer and autumn exist - and that is where I spit out my own winter chest. The winter reaches the surface of my chest in the form of a liquid secreted by the salivary glands of my mouth, crosses the epidermis, the dermis, the hypodermis, to invade this object which I have called my body. You see, this is my fault and I will never be able to get out of this preamble. The auricle, the external auditory canal, the tympanic membrane, the Incus hammer, the stapes, the cochlea, the vestibule of the ear, the external meatus, the tonsils, the cranial region, the diaphragm, the sternum, the viscera, the hypogastrium, the lumbar region, the buttocks, the sacrum, the ilium, the ischium, the pubis, the liver, the humerus, the tibia, the fibula, the jugular, and those anatomical areas that I do not know will never be able to flower as a result of not wanting to shed the viral winter toward my hands - it would be so easy to capture it on my extremities and go to the sink to discard of it - its gardens will never be able to bloom.

There is still another possibility. Maybe spring is pressing my neck with one hand from within. Maybe it's two hands. Maybe it made a pact with winter. Maybe the second hand I feel is winter; that's why I feel like I'm losing air. That's why I feel like I'm dying.

The Newspaper Reporter

by Gloria Piper Roberson

Guadalupe Johnson? Yes, I knew her. We grew up together in the same apartment complex. Chicago. South side. We chewed each other's bubble gum. We cut our fingers with a paring knife to be blood sisters. We devoured Chicken Feet Soup and Chocolate-Beet Cake.

High school? She was the ace of numbers but I out-read her. She did my math homework while I wrote her book reports. That is how we leapfrogged through school. We had nicknames too. She called me Glory B and I called her...

College? Sure, we were friends during college although she began to stray like a yard worm. You know, she dug herself a deep, dark, dirty, tight hole. It was too bad because she always talked about the freedom clouds and airplanes had. You can't fly when you've buried yourself!

Friends? She had them all right. However, they were not what I would call friends. I called them dirty rags. They sopped up any goodness she might have had, and then rung her out whenever and wherever they wanted until she was dry of herself. She became a turtle shell.

She had one child.

Of course she married. It's what some girls believe they are made for—servitude. In her case it was indisputable servitude. Did she stay married? No. There are only so many bones on the outside to break before something on the inside cracks.

Drugs? Plenty. Who didn't? Well, I didn't but you don't want to know about me. Pain pills $40 a pop! She was pill poor. Pay for them? How does any woman pay for drugs when user-claws are scraping their insides? With herself.

When did I see her last? We lost touch years ago, years ago. I knew she cleaned herself up then took a wild chance at getting a job as a parachute tester. Now that is flying! I am happy for her. No, really, I am. Was.

How do you find out anything? You hear it, read it, see it. I don't remember. It doesn't matter. The dots were not for us.

Does it bother me? Yes. It does. I would have liked to have seen her face-to-face again rather than see her picture in the *Shawnee News-Star* and read of her deeds as the oldest of three women parachute testers from Shawnee, Oklahoma whose chute failed over the Arizona testing grounds.

What would I have done if I saw her? I would have shouted her nickname, Lupe J. She would have known it was me. She never let me call her Mother. I never did.

Drugs

by Maximus Ceballos

Air, can you hear the music in the air? Dad's yelling,
Mom's pouting, drugs flowing through my veins to
keep me going, it feels so good. I have no emotions.
All I show is that I have devotion. But the alcohol in
my system keeps me going. It makes me feel numb,
and not so dumb as I'm chasing it down with my
Arizona tea, listening to some crazy oldies. All I taste
is bitterness, but my cigs make me feel ridiculous.
It's so ridiculous it's so good it takes away the
bitterness. It got me light-headed. It's crazy how it's
embedded in my head that cigarettes can have you
dead.

But as girls compliment my hair, all I see is their
stare, sometimes their glare. Sometimes they wink, it
makes me think, and my heart skips a beat...

But sadly it's too late, we pout about how we said we
had faith, as we lie in the grave rotten and dead with
worms squirming through our rotten old heads.

The Me Within

by Kacie Evans

"The best way to keep a secret, is to pretend there isn't one." ---Margaret Atwood.

Even at a young age, I knew I was different.
I recall watching children play. Wondering how such tiny people were capable of making sweet songs and laughter echo through the air. Taking in their movements as their arms and legs danced about like drunken marionettes. Minds focused on only themselves and anything or everything around which could bring them happiness.

Fun.

Fun that I could only dream of.

Fun, I longed for.

Instead I sat in the corner, hoping no one would notice me. Listening to whispers which tickled the very air I breathed and ignoring stolen glances. Praying that I might fade into the sand my fingers sifted through and like that same sand be carried away on a warm summers breeze.

But I knew hope was something I shouldn't bet on. It was simply wasted effort. I had grown accustomed to the fact that things such as fate would never shine their brightness down on my dark existence. So, I watched, and above all, I learned. I learned how to pretend that I wasn't anything like the person I was, and instead more like them. I also knew, above all things, I had to keep the one thing that could destroy me, hidden. The one thing that threatened to break the already frayed hold I had on my world.

My secret.

And so I did. I kept it locked away. But regardless of how tightly I kept my hold, I knew one day the weight of it would be too much to bear. One final drop of water and the dam would burst. Luckily enough (not that luck really had any part of it), with each passing day it had grown easier to hide. Some days, I would find myself caught up in the monotony of life and I would forget, giving myself a hint at peace. Even then, it was the just that. A hint. Nothing could ever make it stop. Bring the voice in my head to a numbing silence.

I lived for silence, moments when I could only hear the blood rushing through my veins, the hum of electricity in the walls, the whisper of air. Funny how loud even silence... can be.

The distant sound of car wheels rolling to a stop broke into my thoughts. Holden was home.

I thought of Holden and remembered how things were in the beginning, an avalanche of memories running through the maze of thoughts in my head. We had worked together. Him, confident and funny and me, a no one, hidden amongst a cacophony of cubicles, dressed simply so as not to be noticed. But despite my efforts of blending in, vanishing into the sea of faces and people I worked amongst but didn't really know, Holden noticed. And he was persistent.

I tried to brush it off, ignore the looks he gave and the words he spoke, but in the end, it felt nice to just be a girl who had caught the eye of a boy.

Normal.

I liked it. No, more than that. I loved it and at the same time it completely terrified me because I knew one day it would all come crashing down and I could only pray it didn't take Holden with it.

Now, three years later here I stand, a house, a mortgage, and a ring resting snugly around the fourth finger on my left hand.

I allowed my eyes to shift from the window above my kitchen sink, to my hands, the now tepid water rolling from my skin. I pulled in a breath and slowly let it out while my fingers found the towel resting on the counter. I picked it up and as it dried the water away, I noted my hands were now trembling.

Even after three years of sharing my life or the life I only allowed my husband to see, I was still scared. I had become very good at listening to a voice I knew only I could hear without looking towards it or more to the point, towards *him.* Thirty-one years of practice will do that. Make you good, but never perfect. I was scared Holden would catch me speaking to *him.* Looking at *him.* Laughing with *him.* And then he would see me for what I really was.

A freak.

Crazy.

God, how I hated the word "crazy."

Crazy was only for people who didn't know they were as such. I knew I wasn't normal but crazy? I turned to *him* as I listened to the car door slam.

"Make him leave," *he* spoke each word with determined purpose. I closed my eyes but not before

I saw *him* standing there, a hard look carved into his handsome face. It was the face of a man I knew loved me, a man who I had grown up with. A man who was the only friend I could be me with. A man I knew only, as Joe. A man I also knew, didn't exist yet was more real to me than the air that occupied my lungs. He never left my side. Was the only constant I had ever had in a world, which could shift, and pivot with the blink of an eye. Pushing past *him*, my feet moved to greet Holden as he walked in and through the front door of our two-story, suburban home.

"Hey Jules," Holden greeted me, his deep, gravelly voice working as a balm to soothe my trembling nerves.

I forced a smile on my face and greeted back. "Hey, how was work?"

I needed normalcy. Craved it.

He threw his keys on the side table with a crash and his long strides brought him to me, where he leaned in, and placed a gentle kiss on my cheek.

Ignoring my question, Holden spoke, and in doing so brought on the events that would forever knock the world, as I knew it, off its axis.

"I'm ready to start a family."

Family.

This was something I had thought about often, but never let myself dream of. It came with too many what-ifs.

What if I couldn't handle the constant attention and focus a child would bring?

What if they turned out like me? I couldn't put anyone through that. Wouldn't.

And then there was the big, what if Joe became angry. He was not the sort of man who you wanted to be around when the anger set in, the jealous anger. I was his and only his or at least that's what he keeps telling me.

I felt not only my body grow tight, but the air in the room shift, and the shift I felt, wasn't good.

"Family?" I repeated. My voice a whisper as the word I dare not speak fell from my lips and crashed heavy on the floor.

I was unable to focus on Holden's response over the envious, angry shouting coming from behind me, shouting that was ringing loudly in only my ears. I squeezed my eyes tight as I felt it happening. The change when my personality took a back seat and Joe's slid in, taking over my body, my thoughts, my entire being. While I felt it happening, knowing it was too late now, I frantically tried to beat it back. Convince him to let me take care of this. Let me choose. But he won. He always won.

"Jules?" I heard Holden's confusion, before the world around me came to a deafening quiet and time stood still.

One, two, three, seconds of nothing and then all faded, to black.

And now here I was. My hands back to trembling and stained pink with the blood that wouldn't come clean no matter how long I stood under the scalding water. I didn't know the details of what happened, but I knew enough.

I sat in the cold hard chair, in the small room whose air smelled of stale cigarettes and day-old coffee. My eyes shifted from my hands and looked deep into *his* satisfied and unremorseful ones. My stomach turned and I feared I might get sick. I swallowed back the thickness and tight feeling in my throat, as I looked unseeing through the mirrored window. I knew they

57

were watching me. I could feel their eyes looking in, burning my skin with their stare and if I listened hard enough, I was sure I could hear them laughing.

Mocking.

I saw my reflection looking back at me and even I didn't recognize myself. The pale skin, the pitiful brown eyes rimmed with a tiredness that never left. The man sitting opposite me, Detective Cooper, or was it Carter, spoke causing my shocked system to jump, the hard metal cuffs cutting into my skin.

"Can you explain to me what happened last night, Mrs. Mckinley."

Mrs.

Everyone knew when a husband got dead it was always the wife. *She probably had enough of his abuse*, they would guess. Or *finally snapped after all these years of hearing she was never good enough.* But they were all wrong. So very wrong.

It was time to let my secret free.

You would think that after years of hiding behind lies and deception I would be scared. But I wasn't scared.

Not anymore. What I was, was relieved. Like I had been carrying the weight of the world on my shoulders and in that instant dropped that same weight at my feet and the freedom felt amazing.

Detective Cooper, growing impatient, somewhat repeated, "Do you know who killed your husband?" My shoulders slumped with relief.

Clearing my throat, I answered. "Yes. It was Joe," my voice, an unwavering murmur.

Not expecting my answer his blue eyes raised to meet mine, the pencil that had been frantically scratching at the small pad of paper stopped.

He blinked. "And who is Joe?"

Deep breath. In and out.

"He's me."

III

Driving Back To Quincy 1954

by Barbara Ellen Baldwin

the red buick rolls along
under a creamsicle sky
rickety barns
holy beauties by the roadside
belong to themselves
sunflowers volunteer here
rising like bright hosannas
the platters sing "twilight time"
with every mile it gets later
no one has lost
anyone dear yet

in a dusty townlet blessed
with bars and churches
neighborhood kids lie
in thick grass looking up
naming jupitor's moons
yellow windows open
familiar rows of welcome
the buick slows then moves on
in the rearview mirror
doors are closing
closing

Wings

by Daniel Sconce

a bird

no larger than the cup of my hand

showed it's trembling wings

as it pressed it feathers against the side wall

of my second floor balcony

its feet pulled up

its beak searching for safety

I saw nothing but death

in it fragile future

it was not for me to mend

beyond my reach I watched

waiting long minutes

for its breath to cease

five - ten - fifteen

then movement

a detectable sound

and it's dot black eyes looked past me

first to the sky then to the ground below

it tried its wings

fluttered

then defying gravity

was at once on the metal rail

a moment later

airborne

it became the sky

I stood to see it go

it is said "his eye is on the sparrow"

while mine judged wrongly

the fate of this fragile fellow

perhaps it was catching its tiny breath

or sick and needed some time

perhaps it had hit my window

and waiting for the pain to wane

whatever placed this tiny bird

on a ledge where safety waited

placed evidence of life's special gift

another chance for wings to lift

The Road Home

by Kacie Evans

How lucky I am to have something that makes saying goodbye, so hard ---A.A. Milne

The sleepy town around him was quiet. Caught somewhere between darkness and dawn, its streets were bathed in a soft hue. With one boot in front of the other he marched on, the sound of gravel and debris crunching beneath his feet. Over his right shoulder was slung a pack, which held all the possessions life had provided him during the last six months neatly tucked away. He wasn't paying any thought as to where his feet were taking him, yet his destination was drawing him in, as though he had been caught up in its spell.

With face cast downward he went on, the echoes of memories he prayed to forget playing on repeat in his mind. In the span of a heartbeat he stopped and for the first time during his journey, paid close mind to where it was.

The familiarity of it all was a comfort to his weary soul like a warm blanket wrapped tightly around him to ward off a chill. His eyes scanned in an effort to take it all in.

The tree-lined street was now beginning to soak up the sun. The last six months he had been drowning in the dreary monotony of earthly colors, brown, tan, beige. But here, it was all too much, the pinks and oranges of sunlight. Greens and blues so bright it almost hurt to look at.

And then there it was.

A place he had dreamed of every night while lying under a foreign sky.

Home.

Forcing a labored breath into his lungs he walked down the weathered brick path he had painstakingly laid himself. Was it four years ago now?

With each step he felt lighter. Freer, like the heavy armor he had encased himself in, was chipping and crumbling away.

He stood now, only a few steps away yet not close enough. He felt so much in that minute his head and heart were dizzy with the emotions warring within him. Overwhelmed with it all he sat down before his legs had the chance to waiver and give way.

He pulled in a deep breath. He used to hear people say that every season had a distinct smell but he had never really given that much thought until now. Freshly cut grass, the sweet smell of the apple, blossoms and wet earth eager to sprout forth life which had been lying in wait.

It was spring.

He smiled for the first time since he didn't know when.

He closed his tired eyes and cast his face upwards towards the sky. The suns morning rays warm on his skin.

The front door creaked open and he turned to see her standing there. She looked even more beautiful than he had remembered. Her bare feet closed the distance between them and she sat alongside him. His soul sighed in knowing its other half was near.

Her soft golden hair fell loosely against her shoulders. He placed his hand over hers, needing to touch her, feel her, prove to himself he wasn't dreaming.

She turned to look at him, her expressive hazel eyes sad and tired.

"I'm so sorry." He said to her, voice thick.

While he was off fighting enemies unknown, she was abandoned to war with those left behind, and that took more courage than he could ever imagine.
Her hazel pools grew wet with tears she fought to hold back.

"I've missed you." She spoke. Those three words a trembling whisper.

He opened his mouth to speak, to tell her he missed her too. To say the words I love you, so that they fell on listening ears and not just written in a letter for her to read or hear through miles and miles of phone lines and static, but a tiny question stopped him.

"Mommy?"

He listened to her pull in a broken breath and in an instant shake away her sadness. But he could still see it. He knew her better than he knew himself. She couldn't hide anything from him.

Seeing her like this he wondered why he had ever gone. Wondered if he had made the right choice. He should have stayed by her side, by *his* side.

"Yeah sweetheart I'm right here." She murmured.

She stood up and turned to see what little Harrison needed. Before the front door slammed shut he heard him ask. "Can I go see daddy now?"

They walked side by side in silence while Harrison skip ran a few steps ahead of them, stopping only to pick every dandelion he saw along the way. He watched his son smile and then laugh as he chased after a butterfly.

He was growing so big and looked just like his mother through and through.

His son stopped and kneeled down in the wet grass to place the now crumpled and wilting flowers down.

He reached for him, needing to tousle his fair hair. Run his calloused palm against his smooth pink skin.

But he didn't.

With his hand held suspended his eyes read the grey stone at his feet.

Harrison James Mckenna
April 5, 1984-May 7, 2017
Father, Husband, Friend

While your war is now over, our fight has only begun.

The world was spinning under his feet.

This couldn't be.

He looked to his son, whose tiny fingers were tracing the words carved there. He looked to his wife and wanted nothing more than to grab her. Hold them both tightly and run, stealing them away with him to wherever it was he was going. But it was impossible now.

With one last glance, he took in the color of his eyes, the curve of her face, the smell of his hair, and etched every detail on his soul so that he would never forget.

Armed only the memories of a life shared and heavy heart, he turned and walked away.

Untitled

by Christine Ingram

your hungry ghosts
cold liquor burns away the memories
sorrowful you could never say goodbye just right
settle for the sun down crepuscular resigning
madness

blank stares
cold and unsettled
awaiting redress which surely
will never come

today is monday and
tomorrow's hands are closed

but rid me of today so that I may love tomorrow
though this instance may be the exception

I swear my fingers will trace the details of your
silhouette long after your figure has ceased casting a
shadow

Courage To Grieve

by Joan Crowe

the drops will not fall
my body will not yield
the cloudy blue sky
will not let me cry

are you here or there?
where is your soul?
you gave me your heart
and I gave you mine

do I have the courage to grieve?
to let the drops fall
to bare my soul
to others?
to me?

Lana

by John E. DeHart

(An excerpt from Post 60)

1979.

Their month-long affair had been reckless. It was closing time at the nightclub where Jay's band played, and as he ambled across the parking lot toward her, even the mid-February chill couldn't cool the heat between them.

At the ripe old age of twenty-four, Lana was the head bartender, and Jay's senior by about a year. *An older woman,* he remembered thinking.

She was wild in the sack, willing, uninhibited, and ready-wet. Her come-hither eyes and intoxicating scent brought orange blossoms to Jay's mind and kept him coming back for more. With Lana practically dripping at his touch, it was the physical chemistry he had always hoped for. Stolen moonlit nights would find them parked on some scenic back road, where, secluded between Saguaros, his station wagon bounced as they fogged up the windows. Since the night she'd invited him to her home and showed him her sleeping little girl, however, his view of Lana had changed. No longer was she merely the willowy redhead who tempted him on nights they worked together; she was a woman who believed in

fate and went for what she wanted. Smart. Classic. A
bubbling well of life.

A shooting star.

He was in awe.

Breaking from the crowd that night, he acted suave,
lighting a cigarette, and strolling toward her car.

"Hiya, kiddo," he said bogie-like. "What's got you in a
pout?"

She smiled slyly. "Come here. I want you to see my
cards."

A big Olds idled out in the parking lot, the woman
behind the wheel giving Jay a sharp stare, but Lana,
unbuttoning her satin blouse with one hand ruled
Jay's attention. He recognized the song emanating
from her radio: *Feels So Good.*

"*Mmm.* Okay, then. Let's see your cards." He gave
them the once-over, and as he handed them back,
her fingers stroked his. "Go for a ride?" She arched
her eyebrows.

Jay's trousers tee-peed.

"Mmm." Lana licked her lips, her eyes on fire.

"Closer."

"Here? You mean right—"

"Closer."

"Oh, I am *so* going to Hell," he whispered as she unzipped him.

Across the lot, the woman revved her engine, flooring the gas, and attracting attention from the far-off crowd. It ruined the moment. Jay squirmed, adjusted himself, and zipped back up.

"Um, look. It's late and, especially tonight..."

She gave him her sad face. "Tomorrow?"

Jay winked. "You're on, doll."

"On top, bottom, upside-down... " She grabbed his waistband. "Kiss me, you tool."

He leaned, and as they kissed deeply, her fingers disappeared down her slacks, then came back up, wet with her sex. She moistened his lips with them, then licked her fingers. Orange blossoms bloomed in

Jay's head as he kissed her again, hard, savoring her wild tongue. "Gawd," he cried out, breaking for air.

"Fucking perfect!"

Smiling seductively, she sat back in her bucket seat, and turned the key. Her engine purring, she slipped the shifter into reverse. "Tomorrow, hotshot."

Snatching the cards from where she'd placed them on the dash, she gave a little wave as she drove off, saying something Jay didn't quite catch.

He watched her disappear down the road. *Do I shine like that to anyone? Of course not,* he told himself. *You're invisible. Remember?*

He realized what she'd been saying, and he blew her a kiss, hoping it would catch up. "Happy Valentine's Day to you too."

The dingbat in the Olds was still staring, but when Jay flipped her off, she popped the clutch, and burned rubber halfway down the frontage road.

"Fugly bitch." He looked around. Everyone had gone.

Crickets and desert sounds resumed. In the stillness, Jay felt Lana's heat lingering in his blood. *I should've gone with her.*

Starting his car, he realized he'd left the radio up.

With you I'm not shy
to show the way I feel.

Door open, left foot on the asphalt, Jay stared as the lyrics sunk in.

With you I might try
my secrets to reveal
for you are a magnet, and I am steel.

"Damn." He lit a cigarette.

Half an hour later, after buying a bag of Puppy Chow from Circle-K, he was going eighty-five down the Black Canyon Freeway, when two State Patrols zipped past, silent as sharks, a Sheriff overtaking them. "Whoa! Those guys are hauling ass!"

Finally home, he parked next to his old Plymouth, fumbled with his keys and let his and Ann's yet unnamed Airedale puppy out. He ate leftovers by the light of the fridge, let the pup back in, brushed his teeth, then slipped quietly between the sheets, careful not to disturb the seemingly innocent. The following day, Ann took the station wagon to work.

Mid-afternoon, knowing the place would be dead at this hour, Jay drove the Plymouth to the club to replace a worn-out drumhead.

Strolling in, he thought about how lucky he was. Most clubs didn't smell like broiling steaks, buttery mushrooms, and baked bread. And to top it off, his band was first-rate on the golden circuit. Deals were in the making.

Life was good.

Jay waved to the pregnant young hostess standing behind her podium. But upon seeing him, she began to cry.

He raised an eyebrow. "Uh, what's wrong, Kelly?"
"Oh, God, Jay, you don't know? I'm so sorry."

"Huh? Sorry about what?"

Kelly's face turned suddenly gray. "It's Lana."

Sirens went off in Jay's head as he remembered the cruisers zipping past last night. He saw Lana's goodbye smile.

"I'm so sorry, Jay. She was... they say it was an accident."

"Where is she? In the E.R.? Which one?" He kicked the podium. "Which hosp—"

She held her hands up. "Jay, lis—"

"Goddammit, Kelly, where *is* she?"

Kelly gripped the podium. "She's dead, Jay, she's dead! It was that friend of hers. God, I can't stop thinking about it! The cops said Lana was stopped at that four-way, over by her house. She just sat there and let that bitch slam into her, Jay! Why? No skid marks! Can you believe that? They said the force sent Lana through the rear window, and her car was propelled..." She groaned, motioning with her hands.

In his mind, Jay saw the Olds impacting Lana's little coup. It looked like dynamite. He felt like a bomb. "...into that telephone pole across the street," Kelly continued. "...and the roof cut..." She couldn't quite deliver the coup de grâce. "Jay, they said it decap—"

The very pregnant Kelly covered her mouth and waddle-ran for the restroom. She did not make it in time.

Jay dropped to his knees. *I should have gone with her.*

Colors seemed leached from life as he weaved the old Plymouth through traffic. At the lonesome road where it happened, he stumbled like a zombie, searching for traces of her in the weeds around the splintered telephone pole.

Something gleamed a few yards away at the road's edge. Scuttling through the sand, he picked up the broken wheel's galloping horse emblem. He went to all fours, and that's when he saw it: caught up in a blue desert flower lay the ribbon she'd tied her hair back with. It was splotched with blood.

Their stolen moments flashed in his mind, and as he caressed the ribbon between thumb and forefinger, he saw her green eyes and could taste her honey kiss.

Out of its envelope, a trampled greeting card lay out on the sand. He recognized it; it was the funny one. As he opened it he heard her sighs, and caught a scent of her that would linger in his soul all his life. *See what you started?*

He fell to his knees, and through tears, saw a lock of her hair flirting with the breeze, not far from his foot. He untangled the auburn strands, brought the ribbon to his face, and breathed her in, burning her into his memory forever. "Go for a ride?" she'd said.

Jay wept openly as the sun moved through the Arizona sky.

Inevitably, his thoughts returned to home. *Ann.* How could he not tell her? She would leave him and rightly so.

The sun was going down; she would be home soon. It was time to face the worst night of his life. So far.

Twenty years later to the day, Jay found himself again with Lana. And although some memories had faded, the heartbreak had not.

He remembered coming out here the night of her burial. There was lightning, branch-snapping winds, and sideways rain, and he had wallowed over her in the newly-turned earth.

But that was then.

Theses days the cemetery looked much different. Peaceful. "Twenty years, kiddo," he told the grass. "I still ache, knowing you're here, Lana. This pain doesn't go away. I know you know. Anyway..."
Birds chirped in the warm afternoon as he searched the sky. "I brought you twenty roses. These things ain't cheap, darlin', let me tell you. Hundred bucks. Don't get me wrong, though, I'd give anything to make you smile... or say hello. If you'd have turned around, Lana, I'd have gone with you that night, no ifs, ands, or buts. Then, either you'd be alive now, or I'd be twenty years dead. I'll never know and I know that's my cross to bear. Things just should've been so different, that's all, and I'm just so sorry, Lana. *So* sorry."

The sun was setting. Again, he said a silent prayer for the little girl who lost her mother on a lover's night. Wiping tears, Jay tucked Lana deep between the folds of his heart where she would remain, safe and forever. "Happy Valentine's Day, sweetheart."
As he left the cemetery, the sinking sun set the desert sky ablaze in golden auburn.

Just like your hair.

Sometimes

by Anabel Watson

you can't fall asleep at night
you think about the ones you know
the ways they've helped you learn and grow
and wonder how they've left your sight
sometimes
it's so hard to leave behind
the pain you felt when trying to care
you were pushed away not even spared
how can you tell what's wrong from right
sometimes
you can only try
to hope that others think back on you
and finally see you cared for them too
there's so much we can realize
sometimes
when you were understood
by people who decided to leave
we all have our reasons to go and breathe
I suppose you feel empty losing
a connection that was so good
sometimes
you can only remember
the people who left you behind
and hope that they were able to find
a world not so entirely blind

Exorcise

by Michael Reed Schooler

don't let your waste
go to shit
don't let your shit
go to waste
utilize everything
that you can
compost it
in post haste
if you want to do nothing
you can
for nil
all your efforts
erased
stomach every bit
of my insight you can
but burn off the excess
and don't mind the taste

In Out Of The Cold Rain (for Ray Carver)
by Mitch McCarrell

This all appeared to me late one night while I sat
thinking of how I had come up out of the cold rain of
another life.

My old life where nothing worked right and too often
it really was always raining, a steady cold Seattle
drizzle draining down from endless gray skies for
days on end.

Second chances, like Ray Carver talked about, after
a long time not even looking for a first chance. I had
sucked up that bitter empty drool so I wouldn't have
to face the other side. Wanting something and maybe
getting it, or maybe not.

Instead I just stood with my back hunched into it,
the blow and downpour, my cap pulled down a notch
or two tighter. The colder the rain, the less anything
worked, the better I liked it, until they left.

The wife and three kids I had discovered too late.
I never walked away from anything until I found
something I figured would end worse.

Second chances, that's what I mean. Even when you
don't deserve one, or maybe especially when you

don't deserve one, when you'd be the last person who should have one.

Those bad old days, that's what I saw now. The too-easy, backward, somewhat embarrassed, awkward glance caught up now in maybe the first good job of a lifetime. And the love of a woman who has made me love the intense blue sky here, the high desert, where the only occasional grief is missing my kids.

Second chances, but more importantly, finding the courage to want one, and the courage to come up out of the cold rain of another life that didn't work to find one here that does and to live it.

Pushing Clay Pots

by Jessica Mitchell

on my balcony I hear
the rustle of dead house-plants
I never watered
that I never liked but you loved
I think of the time you spent out here
watering them
cherishing them like you would a lover
I stand and walk to the railing
where the dry leaves and stubby sticks
sit glaring at me in unspoken accusations
one by one I push them over the side
and listen to the clay pots crash and shatter
on the pavement below
I find myself standing straighter as if a weight is gone
I'm the breeze that caresses my skin
I'm light floating above the surface of the parking lots
where the last shards of you roll along
becoming lost in the oblivion of asphalt

IV

Expectationless

by Anabel Watson

I regret nothing. And who is to say that we must develop in a certain way? Socially. Intellectually. Spiritually. Incessantly changing is our state of being. Our understandings, our morals, our lessons, defining us. Ideas evolve. Connections grow. And maybe this outward expansion is the puzzle built from the sprouts of a seedling of an acquaintance, a particle of experiential snow flowing into a whirlwind of logical and emotional substance that becomes a beautiful ecosystem over time. It starts. Small. And those synergistic interactions we wish we had long ago, couldn't have even been until... now. Now is the time. We didn't lose out; it just took coincidences and networks of mental and literal involvement - evolvement - to arrive at this place. For to embark into a perfect and immediate world would be an unrealistic dream.

Me Money

by Sylvia B.

everything's always about money and power

how many people can I send home today

to save me money

how many people can I make do this so I don't have

to hire anyone else

better yet so IIIII don't have to

everyone one uses and uses

IT'S ALL ABOUT MEEEEEEEEE

what can IIIIIIIII get from YOOOOOUUUUUU

OH I see you are a mat that says WELCOMEEEEEE

the nice people

the good people

have their heads so far up EVERYONE'S ASS

they must love the taste OF FUCKING ASSS

USE AND ABUSE BABY

that is what it's ALLLLL ABOUUUUTTTT

YEEEEEEEEEEE

FUCK EMMMM

I DO NOT GIVE A FUCKKKK because it is all about

MEEEE

MMEEEEE

YOU HEAR

ME ME ME ME ME

FUCK YOU AND ANYONE who gets in MYYYYYY way

yeah? WELL FUCK YOU TOO FUCKER

The Root Of All Deception

by Mike Morgan

money will not make you happy
it's a theory that we've been told

the rich curse their good fortunes
and are bored with cash and gold

let the wealthy bitch and moan
and I will be their minion

but please god
please give me the chance
to form my own opinion

Wishful Thinking: "This One's For The Ladies"

By Jessica Mitchell

I wish last names had nothing to do with marriage.

I wish that I could go back and take the name of the woman who birthed the woman who birthed the woman who birthed me.

But it would just be a man's name.

I wish I could walk down the street in a tube top and a tutu at 3 a.m. and not have to bring a whistle, a weapon, or mace.

I wish I didn't have to teach my daughters how to protect themselves, while your "boys are just boys being boys."

I wish that his catholic mother didn't ask me why I "didn't just take care of it when I had the chance," because my daughter might ruin her son's life.

I wish. I wish, and I wish, and I wish for a world where we didn't ask if she asked for it.

Where we didn't question how much she drank, or what she wore, or whether she enjoyed it.

A physical response to a physical action does not excuse emotional trauma.

I don't hate men. I have brothers, and sons, and lovers. I fall asleep next to a man every night.

But this is not about me. It's about my daughter's daughter's daughter.

What world will she live in?

Will she know to "never go out alone?"

Will she make less than her brother at the same job? Or will she rise above? Will she wear whatever the fuck she wants without the fear of rape? Will her husband take my name? Will she conquer the corporate world in a tutu and ballet flats and never be confused with being a woman "in a man's world?"

Oh I wish, and I wish, and I wish, and I can only hope...

John The Apostle

By Dylan Eichenauer

There was a storm brewing on the horizon. Or was there? Or would there be? John might have well been able to tell, had he the inclination for a more focused observation of the setting on this particular occasion, but other thoughts were about:

Could it be that I love him? What is right? What is good? Am I good? I am great. I am the best. I do what he intended. I do what is natural. How could I be better? I believe in his greatness. Believe in his greatness, His Decree. That is what they taught me, what they enforced. Strictly. This is how I know that this is what is natural and best. That is what they told me. That is what they taught me for so long.

Were they right? There certainly was no possibility of anything else being the case, they were not wrong. There was no space for doubt. They were not to be challenged. At any rate they were teaching me what was natural and best.

Though, what is this feeling? I love him. This is how I know that they were not right. He was greatness.

And in this moment, neurons, synapses, circuitry ablaze—in his mental space emerged a dense, tenuous network of memories, images, smells, tactile sensations, sounds, intuitions, ideas, thoughts swirling ebulliently, elegantly reforming poignant experiences, and forming poignant experiences in the process of rekindling, and reforming those past experiences, that were so certain, specific, integral, undeniable, and concrete. John formed himself, he was no longer past, for John, he was clearly a part of his present. It brought a brilliant happiness to him.

John was standing on the shore. Looking out over the mass of water. It brought him an unexpectedly immeasurable peace. It gave him something that the rest of his life was lacking. His freshly cleaned suit, shined shoes, matching belt, secured watch, proper tie, combed hair, juxtaposed with the simple, undeniable beauty of the existing environment, encapsulating him at the current moment.

What was that? Strange thoughts. I should stop that. I should stop this. There is nothing wrong with me. There is nothing wrong with how I live. I am naturally great and the best. I cannot be wrong in my beliefs. I don't have time. I need to get back to business; I need to get back to work. This is how I support my family. That is what they taught and enforced. And they were right. There is no space for doubt, to challenge. Why am I standing here?

John was impelled towards movement. He knew he couldn't stand there any longer. Standing there longer would result in examining thoughts. Thoughtfulness, conclusions, actions emerging from those conclusions. He did not have time, with the many events he had been present for, paperwork that needed attention, and review, attending to appearances, everything to keep him busy. Business was important to John. Pushing damp sand out of his way. Leaving firm footprints. Leaving the lightly, lapping, mass of water. Contending with wind, blowing against his appearance. He strode hurriedly towards his Ford.

There it is, my clean, reliable, black Ford. It is integral to my business. It allows me to support my family. Father worked for Mr. Ford. He always told me what a great man Ford was. And why should I doubt that? My Ford affords me my perfect life. We ought to be thankful for this invention of his.

John liked to remind himself of that fact. He loved his truck, for it allowed him to be industrious, lent itself greatly to his business. John reveled in the feeling of control brought to him by the directed placement of the key in the ignition and the assured start of the engine.

He drove, distractedly, through traffic, towards his office, reminding himself of his importance, and affirming himself in his ability to act. Acting, without doubt, in his pursuit of greatness.

I am great because this is how I was destined to be. It is what they wanted. It is what he wanted. It was their will, together. Now, people ought to be grateful for me. For my reliability and power. They should act accordingly and get out of my way. Are they not aware of my importance?

He often thought like this on his drives to his office. Though the sentiments were clear, forceful even, he never considered them to be derived or intended maliciously. For John it was simply a matter of the importance of his business.

He arrived at his office not a minute late and his assistants greeted him upon his entering. "Hello, Mr. Fraus," seasoned with a commonplace placation. He kept up with appearances. Smile for smile. John knew he was great. He went quickly to his office, closed the door, sat, gave great consideration to his idea of keeping busy, but actually did nothing. The rest of the day went through its mundane motions, his assistants and staff doing their work. Serving his greatness.

The day-end neared and something was burning. John felt an imposing discomfort and caressed one of his suited arms. He bothered with his tie and realized a fine layer of sweat had replaced the feeling of his fresh, clean suit. He stood up. He began pacing.

Is something burning? What is this feeling? This peculiar smell? The fragrance is familiar.

Exasperatedly, John rushed to the door that usually remained closed. Out in plain sight, amidst all desks, paperwork, and staff, was someone remarkably similar in appearance to him, enrobed in an inferno. He could hardly tell the features for the intensity of the flame burning away flesh with fervor.

They can see this, the sheen in their eyes. The fine smirks at the corners of their mouths. Why is no one doing anything, saying anything, when it is clear that they know? What is wrong with me? There is nothing wrong with me, with how I live. I am greatness. That's what they told me, taught me, enforced. How they wanted me to be. They were wrong. Adam. That was his name. Why was it so hard to remember? I love him. He is here with me, but I miss him. I miss the physical. I miss the touch of his delicate hand. The caressing of my body against his, slim, but solidly sculpted.

Don't Worry Uncle Sam, I'm Still A Dandy Yankee Doodle

by Michael Reed Schooler

some things will surely never
be all right
the long painful strain through those
bleak dead-end nights
and eternal mornings with feelings
of spite
a brain thinking backward
a sun far too bright
thinking "jesus christ" what was I
drinking last night
was it root beer and gin
or heineken light?
one thing is for sure
I'm still high as a kite
as I stumble to try and just
turn out the light
and fall onto blankets
of red blue and white

Quislings

by Eric W. Fotherby

I find it difficult to accept political opinions from
pretentious, over-privileged, and over-indulged,
inefficacious Hollywood aristocrats. It appears that
they cannot even manage to execute their own back-
slapping ceremonies with a proper decorum of
respectability anymore.

What has been, and is well-known, and is also world-
renowned to everyone as the Oscars, is that it is now
being ruined by the over-emotional, altruistic,
ridiculously simplistic, melodramas of the ersatz
elite. The methodically repetitive, emotional diatribes
that keep cascading forth from the stage in an on-
going effort to project guilt-ridden complexes upon
the television audience has now become
disingenuous and repugnant to even the most loyal
of fans for this event. The extreme-leftist liberal point
of view is relentlessly and inexorably foisted upon all
of Middle-Class America; who are by the way the very
ones who pay their bills and their taxes and finance
all of their drug-induced fantasies.

The Academy Awards Ceremony has now become an
enormous travesty too obnoxious to tolerate for most
of the public suffering through mediocre Prime Time
viewing these days. Hollywood's massive, licentious,

99

amoral, depraved, and lewd effort at indoctrinating the Middle-Class of America with messages of libertine and promiscuous sexual behavior while proselytizing for Global Government, Media Control, Wall-Street foreign ownership, and a Washington D. C. that is being controlled by foreign billionaires has now proved to be truly unacceptable to us, the unwashed masses, the proletariat, those of us who are the real people of America today.

Weeping, whining thespians with their spittle-laced words spewing and spilling forth from lecherous lips espousing aggrandizement of lobbyist-outsiders and foreign carpetbaggers only makes all of their remonstrance and their expostulation just nothing more than rhetoric and dogma that is now falling upon the deaf ears and the hardened hearts of the good and decent people of this country!

Second Amendment, Third Round

by Mike Morgan

I've no desire to own a gun
it's simply not my thing
I get my food from grocery stores
and let the wild birds sing

there is no one I want to kill
no woman child or man
and I can think of cheaper ways
to put holes in a can.

I have the right to make this choice
but my rights end with me
for if I tell you what to do
then none of us are free

so you may trample through the woods
armed for cans or game
and keep a handgun for defense
to me it's all the same

politicians love to meddle
but let me tell you brother
freedom is a present that we give to one another

Just a Thought

by Tyler Burlingame

jackhammers sound

an awful lot like gunfire

in the distance

I wonder

if a war could be won

through the sonic theater

I'm honestly surprised

we don't have intimidation

plumbed and tapped into our homes

Racially Diverse

by Mike Morgan

I wish I belonged to an ethnic group

generic "caucasian" is weak

but having examined my family tree

I'm starting to feel more unique

I'm welsh and I'm english - a viking - a jew -

chickasaw - cherokee - creek

and those are the ones certifiably sound

while others I don't care to seek

so I will create a minority name

and label it "eurojuni"

making me worthy of favor and fame

no longer an average guy

affirmative action becomes my new friend

benefits cannot deny

for we are more rare than hispanics or blacks

statistics cannot ever lie

then again if I follow our family tree

back far enough into time

we all become brothers

both you and me

the differences not worth a dime

everyone comes from the same ancient roots

back to a mutual mother

giving us reason to forage ahead

accepting and loving each other

All Us Silly Taxpayers

by Michael Reed Schooler

the clock has now

turned upside-down

my face is fixed

into a frown

whisky lockjaw

does not drown

making my way

all day

across town

sleepwalking

guided

by all of the sound

snow tires

crunching away

at the frozen ground

V

Silence

by Sylvia B.

on good days I am human

I forget things

I smile

I laugh

I hug

I touch

on bad days I go in a haze

blurry

cannot see

copy of a copy

what's real what's not

shut down

don't eat

black out

don't breathe

silence

Dead Animals And The Very Old.

by Jesemynn Cacka

What do old people think when their animals die?
I mean really, *really* old people. Like, can't check the
mail without almost dying old.

Do they see a foreshadowing of death, gripping their
face with boney white knuckles, or just another
goldfish to flush down the toilet?

Nothing money can't fix in the exact same make and
model.

I once had an aunt who bought like five Airedale
Terriers and named them Maggie, but not at the
same time, only after the current Maggie died. One
after another, after another, another, nother, other.

How many me's are there to replace the one before?
In how many makes and models? What do old people
think when their animals die?

Untitled

by Dylan Eichenauer

amidst women of the night
my crimes inlay a blatant fright
against I no throat dost fight
slick and smooth from left to right
upon the walls dost cruor splash
eternally my knife they wear your lash

oh notice how the figure falls
I tatter them shallow sickly dolls
about the torso blunt force mauls
the face wears bruises midnight palls
my gift forthright humanity adores
my bloody artwork treasured pours

eviscerated bowels slipping forth
stripped from bodies lacking worth
ripped entrails incur my mirth
my design entails a cherished birth
gory acts do abash
eliciting sorrow ever rash

I flee by gentle coruscation
trembling violently
pure elation
by the day I hold my station
detectives bearing consternation

I will most certainly strike again
more carrion to feed the den

these naïve streets are never safe
dear morality here is my heart!

Growing Panes

by Michael Reed Schooler

all which was once

unsuppressed

became a shame

when life regressed

and knowing more

knew so much less

just blame our claim

of all duress

from thane is gained

more reign

in jest

now "karma" fully anoints

their quest

with sorrow mind

or morrow breast

neglects designs

we fail this nest

through

out the blinds

you'll read your best

for words behind

arrange to bless

The Void Knows

by Rachel Lynn Lippert

the black void amidst her waters of blue out of
whence came the light did spew

but that which once was fair and bright turns dull
forth with the coming night

thine eyes took glimpse of other side and the
emptiness she dare not hide

yet fear bit at my heal of mind and the secret fell
deeper from the gloom inside

I hid among the rainbow tune and the feasting sirens
of her room

but the aisle she walked faded in and dwindled out
until at last she hummed turning me about

cast out thy demon dwelling below to ignore the seed
that she would sow

brave travelers come to pay their peace but those
waters they churn until she sleeps

treading lightly as she peeks the dark chasms
queries she doth keep

111

I find myself of lost and alone this blackest of islands
I've never known

shall I float off into confession hesitate not she
knows my apprehension

how so can she discern without phrase this
dimension the void possesses in the coming daze
but I must capture the mystery she clenches strong
and I stare deeper as the wholeness lingers on

I love you
I love you
I love you

more so much more passing onto me like the rays of
the sun she set me free

and now I am haunted by her waters of blue and the
black void out her thoughts she did spew

with one single stare inside my being she knew the
coming the going she was all seeing

then the bond vanished behind soft rose petal doors
and the poison tiptoed across the floors

forget I will never that abyss of sweet time
love devoted precious soul forever of mine

The Heart

by Holly Crawford

Laying in this dark, quiet room, watching the shadows dance across the wall. I find myself feeling, falling, and wanting more.

The desire for our closeness on my mind, wishing you were here, to feel your embrace, your touch, your closeness.

Thinking of this steals my breath away.

These feelings are beyond my control.

Love is patient, love is kind, and love is more than a feeling that goes away. Love is there to stay.

So here in this moment, these feelings, as wide as a deep blue sea, no limit to the exhilaration of what it feels.

I carry on.

The sun is fading and I pick up my books and off I go. Every time I feel the longing, I will stop and quietly smile with a deep sigh.

This seems like yesterday.

Hearing the teapot screaming, I pull my cozy blanket up over my chest. I look up, sip my warm tea, and smile as I see the beautiful bright stars shine!

Vibrant Orange

by Jessica Mitchell

you touch me with hands of silk

leaving behind the scent of your cologne

it stays with me for hours

I still feel your lips on my ear moments before you

trace lines down the nape of my neck

you leave me breathless and I shiver from your hot

breath in my ear

the saxophone from the jazz floating through the air

cocoons us in our little world

your hands slide down my arms

and I am frozen from the gentleness of you

you slay me with whispered words that leave my

heart pounding

days go by and I go back to that moment

when you're pressed against me

arms wrapped around my waist

no thoughts no fear

just a single moment of clarity

of bliss like the rising sun

filling the sky with orange hues

no painter can define

tango dance of rising fire

that bursts into flames

bright blue in the darkness

oh how I long for your touch again

Untitled

by Eric W. Fotherby

everyone misunderstanding

nobody caring

no longer sharing

living alone in the dark

emotions withheld for fear of the emptiness that

spreads to the skies

all of us asking why and I don't want to know when

it's my time to die!

my cup runneth over with love

my life has been blessed from the heavens above

always carrying the guilt of such an effortless life

very little strife

carefully planning very safe landings

it's been years since I've risked all of the tears

too old to risk chances of the heart

the heart no longer controls the fear

fear controls it!

pain is the whip

that keeps snapping against old backs

as they move down the road towards father time

Dreaming Of A Darkness

by Mitch McCarrell

In late fall, close to evening and the end of love, we
drove the old Ford upriver, wanting to cross Crum
Canyon over the mesa—one last road to show you
before you left. Snow began falling lightly, too early
in evening for headlights. The dirt road changed
colors (brown to white) as it led us higher, the pickup
skittering between ruts and fresh snow.

We both seemed unsure of ourselves at every turn
and corner, but I would not turn back, and at the
last rise, the sky loomed blue to purple, the tires
spinning, finding the summit.

Where the road was cut, opening in the steep slope,
I stopped, and you ran back the way we came. The
snow came thicker down from the falling darkness
that settled quickly now.

I checked over the truck for cut tires, broken springs,
any failing. When I could look at you, you ran toward
me, laughing, your shoes gliding in the packed snow
of the tire tracks. Falling snow became small boats of
white, rocking home, touching your hair and
shoulders, as darkness veiled the world. Holding you
against me, I could smell your hair. I opened my
mouth and tasted wet snow. To my left, past

the blackness of your hair, through the ordered methodical white snow falling through coming darkness, down a slope that became a canyon, the river lay in crooked folds, so flat, black, and silent, miles away, its waters and whirlpools leveled by distance and dark.

I wondered if what I saw, the space between objects, the ending I couldn't imagine, was real. And years from it, on a morning like this, where city traffic winds too quickly about itself, when a job would ask otherwise, and promises lead other places.

I sit dreaming of a darkness that love held off,
of snow that falls even now, into the dark muskiness
of your hair. Of your arms holding me on the edge of
that road, so far above the river and the pulling
darkness.

Ugly Faces

by Jesemynn Cacka

in the belly of a skeletal beast

fires made of driftwood

shooting the shit

chasing the moon

smokes between knuckles

let's dance to that tune

make an ugly face and I'll show you mine

dizzy feet

hazy minds

drowned out laughter by the rush of night

you light yours and I'll light mine

I got a story if you got an ear

my father was a bastard ya hear?

light em if you got em and I got mine

bright eyes - magnet feet - traverse up the spine

the sun's almost up and we got things to do

even though I'd rather spend my time

making ugly faces at you

You Were Like A Spirit Long Before You Became One

By Gloria Piper Roberson

It is out of the dailiness of life that one is driven into the deepest recesses of the self ---Stanley Kuntz

While relaxing in the breezeway swing today, I thought about you and how you would appear in this swing—your feet rocking you—to watch me tend our vegetable garden.

I would sense your presence, look up to find you smiling. You would invite me with a pat on the swing seat. I would pull off a dirty glove and hold your hand and we'd sit and gab of garlic and beets until I'd return to the patch, energetic as a child.

I would look up again to see you. Like now, you had vanished.

Seasons

by Michael E. Bull

snow falling on hemlocks

on a brisk winter's day

in the deep woods

I walk along the path I have trod before

to a place I know well

it was here she said goodbye

a blink a turn of the head

when I looked again she was gone

leaves falling on hemlocks

on a chill autumn morning

the world has turned

seasons have passed

and I am left with memories

she has taken flight

the marker bears her name

the name of the one I love

have loved will love till time freezes

like my heart

cold as stone

like the ground beneath my feet

above her face - her hair - her eyes

her form - her mouth

so still so cold

I walk the lane

between the woods

back to the cabin

the fire is warm

my heart so cold

it is cold here

in the woods

in the autumn

in the time after

I can go to her

but she cannot come back to me

perhaps in winter

when the snows kisses the hemlocks once more

it will be time

a journey made a threshold crossed

a kingdom entered a world exited

a hand to touch her lips to caress

it will be warm there

in the spring

amidst the flowers

in the meadow

beneath the blue

beside the hill

beneath the clouds the sun

where memories

like burning logs upon the hearth

warm the soul
now those memories
like icicles
hang upon my heart
but when spring comes
the ice will break
winter's chill will pass
and I will see her smile
as welcomed as the sun after rain

snow falling on hemlocks
on a brisk winter's day
that froze the world

leaves falling on hemlocks
on a chill autumn morning
a heart frozen before winter

I will wait while winter lingers
soon will come the spring

       * * *

sunlight on flowers
on a warm spring day
a touch of a hand
a brush of her lips on my cheek
winter has passed
I am home

A Last Word

by Mitch McCarrell

and so the first word you have
comes like this
maybe a half hour
after you've admitted to a woman
who's really not your wife
that you can't be sure of the date
of your mother's birthday
the end of this month or
the beginning of the next

the first word that your mother
will be dead in a day or maybe two

and the first word you have
concerns her last days
their quality
a strange word at this point
it's late evening when these calls come
somewhere between dinner and bedtime
these death calls
you can label them
dark messages that will end someone's life
calls the living make to discuss someone
slipping off into another place
my mother
there isn't anything to say

not on the phone or to one another
and not to her if I were there
because she doesn't understand our words
anymore

so maybe the first word
is for the woman she's become
these last few years there in that rest home

but this first word is also the last
for the laughing woman who raised us
hated the wind
spoke to birds
and cursed weeds
and the fleeting days
all of that lifetime's ago
now she's just a stone
worn away
by the diminution of time
and finally
by this last word

Starlight

by Jessica Mitchell

seeking clarity in the stars
as I look up into the darkness
massive waves crash against the shore
and I dig my feet a little deeper in the sand
I define my life by passing colors
in the ever changing breeze
the incessant spinning of lights
as I circle the outside peeking in

I breathe through the noise of the day
through the blur of people running
I praise the setting sun with my hands reaching so
far into the sky I surpass the rising moon
she's with me now

in the distance caw of the sea gulls
the buoys chiming near the harbor
I see her eyes reflected
in the twinkling starlight that breaks
against the surf

I don't believe in heaven nor a god
that rips babies from fertile wombs
that takes babies' breaths while they dream
leaving mothers' arms empty

but I do believe

in her curls

in the sweet musky scent of newborn flesh

of her coos and mews between gulps

of liquid gold from my breast

she is every starlight night when I walk the beach

miles and miles before I sink into the

cold wet sand

I whisper her name into the darkness

Twilight

by Debra K. Rodgers

twilight's golden eye unveils a vivid scene

but only for a breath - a lover's sigh

of ardent blush and blaze I've only dreamed

my youth - a ghostly figure - shimmers nigh

I float as though a thought - a breathless grace

weightless as a bride's fragrant bouquet

the tall cool grasses sway and reach to trace

their quiet correspondence on my leg

I wish I could escape into its charm

an otherworld of rose beyond the blues

and never fear again to come to harm

embraced - a cherished child - among its hues

for now I'll be content to know it's there

flirtatious as a coy lover's care

Ancient Love Song

by Gloria Piper Roberson

come into my evening
says the woman of my dream
so I fly to her like sea to shore
like an arrow shot from cupids bow
like days are gone and nights no more
I fly

come into my boudoir speak
her warm green liquid eyes
so I race to her like bees to buds
like camels on the gobi sands
like she is air and breath and life
I race

Stay here with me
she purrs through pouting begging lips
so I stay as lovers do
like music on the ear
like pure honey on the tongue of the hummingbird
I stay

in light of day
I see a lover's web
and me entangled in its knotted thread

Shower Mates

by Jesemynn Cacka

"Who do you think you are?"

Dumbstruck, I kept quiet, and chased the distaste
with light beer.

He was gone before I could truly show him.

Doubtful there would be a second chance, but I've
mulled it over day after day since then.

With a shared bowl and cold Rainier, I would say,
"I think I'm the kind of woman who shares a shower
with a spider because he isn't bothering anyone."

A Death Between Lovers

by Paiton Mabery

I don't know if you'll feel like reading anytime soon.

But I'm slowly fading as I write this. I've found myself consumed by fading memories, as if you're in the room. I feel my breath ponder then silently leave.

If you only knew the hell I'm living, if you could only conceive.

But if you read this I hope it makes you sad. You see, feeling pain is something; when it's all you seem to have.

I hope each time we kissed it would make you mad that it could always be the last. You never really know, when I drive home alone, if I'm really getting home.

I've thought of things to tell you, while lying in my bed. I've wrapped them up, sealed them up, and tied them with a bow. But if you knew everything my brain was turning, maybe then you'd know what it really feels like when you think you've found your soul.

Deep inside my chest it was placed under my bones, and I only felt it stutter, but it's enough for me to know, that when I'm driving far away from you, I wont be driving home. A piece of me has been left behind, a piece I can't let go. And when I get to where I'm going, I know it won't be home.

I know that I am only happy when I am truly alone, because the walls in this house are only crumbling down. The nails in the walls are all pouring out.

I'm not home at all as I sit in my bed. The only place I feel welcomed is when I go inside my own head.

I hope you cried over me as many times as I did you. I thought I'd lose my eyes, they'd just fall out and give too, but they stay rotting like my heart did when I moved on and moved too.

I hope that you hated every color that you saw, if you saw them at all, because it was hard to see something beautiful with a view so small.

And I miss you, and I hate that too. I hate that every second our lips caught a breath it was ended way too soon.

Cause I remember you softly breathing, your caring tune.

Cause I remember the way it felt to be pressed against you.

Every moment, gone, too quick. Sometimes I feel like I just want to end this shit.

Cause you were all I ever wanted, I wrote it in my skin, and when you left I think my heart did.

There's this hole inside my chest. And it is torn and bruised and barely new. Its hard to deal with at best, and it reminds me so much of you. And it hurts like you hurt me, when you couldn't be there too.

Cause you had to get your head right, and I couldn't be near you.

Cause this hole, this spot you've dug out of me. It's all I ever look at. It's all I ever see.

And it sees me every night and when I wake its just as fresh. I contemplated suicide, but I never do my best in things I know I'm good at. I always seem to fail.

Cause I'm too busy keeping track of the things that will prevail. But bursting from the ashes it's not a fable tale of a girl who's broken hearted and a boy that's forever missed.

133

A death between lovers, when *the pair* became, *just two*. At the funeral I brought flowers, I brought them for you.

Blackened Guts

by Sylvia B.

rip open my chest you'd find nothing

but some busted up black lungs

a punctured heart seeping black slime

no sign of life here

skeletons in my closet

cobwebs in my chest

completely numb

scared of what this numbness brings

scared to feel

so undeserving of this life

what a waste

waste of space

waste of time

wake up get up

days just drag on

my shadow slumps behind me

and we do not want to be here

lump in my throat

no thump in my chest

no hip to my hop

slime in my veins

not here

not there

not anywhere

stop asking questions

no answers here

VI

Future's Door

by Daniel Sconce

shred the dictionary

standing sentry

over your motives and your mission

silence your cherished definitions

pound apart the frame of language

the joists of verbs

the studs of syntax

the structure of self will collapse

your component parts suddenly useless

a pointless bed of nails

collect the shreds

the brokenness

the fading light of right and wrong

toss in faith's foolishness and fiction's excess

weave what remains of yourself

into a coarse welcome mat

exhale what is left of your ego

and lay flat before future's door

yes you might have become more than this

yes you might have missed a chance

but of the soles that pass across you

some may feel a welcome home

some may learn to dance

Hidden Cave

By Robert "Cougar" Penhaligon

I almost didn't make it to Mount Shasta this year for two reasons. The first was "the three week crud" was on me for the third time this year! A constantly dripping nose does not make for a good 11 hour drive to the mountain. After a days delay I could not resist going anyway. When I was 8 hours away I discovered my main drive belt was falling apart, strip-by-strip. Unshaken, I made it into Weed the next morning and found not only a new belt, but a mechanic willing to put it on right away. I could have been stranded for a couple of days easily in some of this 600-mile terrain. I was very grateful for my unusual fortune.

I then had a dream of flying onto the heads of the Gods (20 foot marble statuary). Helios (He-Lion) woke and was very angry and vengeful yet I felt a tremendous amount of power and freedom about being able to do that during my escape flight from the awakening Gods. How dare I stand on the heads of Gods!

Tuesday, 16 Sept 2008, I went in hiking at the 7000 foot level of the mountain from Panther Meadows. I have been here many times in the last 10 years and decided to follow my nose off the beaten path to find something different. I discovered two false caves near each other but with barely enough room to sit in. These were huge boulders that had come off Rock Buttress and crashed onto other boulders and sealed off at three of the four ends, leaving an opening. I did some Tibetan practice in the best one and realized I could push some dirt around to make a straighter sitting room and maybe at a later date I could build some stone into the windy side portal, making it more cave-like and secure.

I found the camp host, who had come back into Panther on Wednesday, and got his permission to work this cave on a future visit only because when we had met last year, he got to know we were similar in our desire to keep the mountain sacred. This camp host has been coming to the mountain for 20 years and knew it pretty well. Inspired by my discovery, I was encouraged to ask him if he knew of any real caves on the mountain. If he hadn't explored one himself, he works with two local tribes when they do ritual on Shasta and they must know from the centuries old mythology of magical entry into the mountain. After all, when I was fast asleep here in 1987 I fell into the heart of Mount Shasta and woke up clamoring through dream rock and dream dirt to get back out to fresh air.

His answer was that he knew of the couple of false caves but not of any real caves, neither did the Wintu nor Katuk Elders, but thanks to perfect timing, recently someone came through the camp with a photo of what appeared to be a cave in the far distance of a meadow obscured by trees! It had been recent enough that he hadn't explored for it yet, but will go soon. I realized that a Buddhist Adept may have found it 5 years ago since he had camped down there where no one is officially permitted to camp. It is a protected delicate wilderness.

18 Sept 2008, I headed off for Waika Meadows, an hour and a half hike in. Just as the trail enters the meadow, I veered right and went down stream where there was a faint trail off the beaten path. I was surprised at the activity of the 35 foot waterfall that is not on any map for the public to know about (it was known by word of mouth). Most people travel to the popular upper waterfall beyond Waika, "Spring Tub." I continued down to the point where I had gotten five years ago when I ran out of time looking for that Buddhist wise man out here. I could *just* see some of the Lower Waika Meadow from there. This was where he was said to have been.

As I carefully traveled down closer, I could hear a male and a female talking to each other and laughing but I couldn't make out any words. I stopped to listen and the voices stopped. Strange, there was no one there when I entered the Lower Meadow.

Something opened up deep inside me. I continued to travel down further only to discover yet another meadow (but more temptingly tree shaded) no one had mentioned and realized it as a perfect spot to camp next year. No footprints, no people, no sun-beating heat.

I came back up to the Lower Meadow and looked through my binoculars from the best position, only to excitedly see a cave perhaps 30 feet from the top of the East end of Red Butte, obscured by a tree top smack-dab in front of the middle of the mouth. Any other position on the open meadow obscures the cave completely. Now I had done what I set out to do: verify the existence of the cave.

I was to head back to Upper Waika to finish my day in bliss in that holy place and report back to the Forest Service but something held me back from leaving Lower Waika. I realized in the waiting of another whole year to return, the true existence of this cave would gnaw at my mind. I reflected on my recent reading of how after repeated attempts, Ian Baker and Ken Storm had finally "discovered" the 108-foot Hidden Falls (the portal to legendary Shangri-La) in the five mile (hither-to-impossible to explore) gap of the Tsangpo River in 1998. This place was found in the Hidden Lands of Pemako, east of Lhasa in Tibet. It was a place protected by local spirits, fierce nature, and by Padmasambhava himself from all but the most deserved. According to Padmasambhava's revelations, Pemako is the most dangerous as well as the greatest of all the (beyul) hidden lands, "a celestial realm on earth." In song it is known as "a pure realm for the Buddhas, of past, present, and future, a place where fortunate beings can find enlightenment. Those without pure perception will have no chance here."

Ian Baker, a 20 year+ Tibetan scholar and mountaineer from Kathmandu spent some time at the point of imminent discovery in his book writing about sacred caves to Tibetan Practice. This is what I had last read in his book, in his last chapter just before I reached Shasta. I knew at this very moment now that this is what I have been setting myself up to do over the years of exploring out here on Shasta. This was my calling on the mountain.

I set my pack down, leaving my water and all behind, and traveled up the right side into the forested buttress. Again, I heard the singsong voices of a man and woman not far from me, up in the air above the enclosed dale. This time, I was ready to know this was the Spirit of the Mountain calling me,

142

initiating me, welcoming me into unexplored sacred space in perfect synchronicity of physical location. I thanked the mountain and intuitively joined with it more deeply. Then, in the only sandy area between the forest and the solid rock I discovered not only deer tracks but for my first time on the mountain, some bear tracks. I had heard yesterday that a bear is here on the east side. Great, a cave and a bear, makes sense.

After an hour total, I found myself at the last dangerous level before the summit. Loose rocks under my feet had slipped out, crashing 100 feet and more below me. Before my eyes lay a most vertical climb. I crossed over to the left to find myself just under the cave opening, but it wasn't there. I went over further but could see now the meadow was out of site. If I had climbed to the top, I wouldn't be able to see the cave. How did I miss it? I went back to the middle. Those three rocks in 3D and shade could look like a cave through binoculars! Is this all it is?

Frustrated, I scrambled down the steep grade and straight back into the far side of the meadow. There it is! How did I miss it? I am running out of enough daylight for my return trip to Panther. I don't care! I will take a full frontal ascent and veer off where I must. I dug my cougar claws in and pressed forward (I was wearing my Roz cougar shirt). I kept my eyes

143

trained on the tree directly at the top above the cave. That tree did not disappear from sight for long.

About half way up I had to veer left around an overhang and then fight my way back to center just under where the cave should be. My hiking shoes of 20 years burst open at both Achilles heals. At once the cave appeared! Unbelievable! I paused and joined my palms in triple gesture. As I approached the entrance I paused and joined them again. For a brief moment I could see two figures inside! Were these the two I had heard? But they were now not seen as real, more like statues or carvings? I forgot totally about the bear!

No wonder why I missed the cave on my first attempt. It was only 15 feet from the top and not the 30 feet it seemed to be from the distance. I had been just under the ledge sighting it. I entered the cave. The figures were gone! A trick of my imagination or...

I positioned myself in the center of the cave facing out. My perfect meditation spot! I noticed very little moss on the cave walls but no bat guano. It wasn't a dark deep cave. There was a little growing fern in there. I was going to take mental measurements of the depth but was distracted from that task when I found I was struck with horror at a new discovery. I am no Geologist but at the base of the cave was a

splintering crack at both sides where it looks
like it shifted and was caught again but moved
enough to cause some rock to crumble and fall out
over the ledge it was sitting on. There were more
cracks along the sides and they were all at 40 degree
angles.

This cave was not sitting flat, nor was it safe. My
horror increased when I could see the rock in front of
me at the mouth of the cave was shattered into slabs
like huge teeth that were all facing in, in-other-
words, if the cave shifted again at that 40 degree
angle, one couldn't run out ahead of it without
volleying out over the ledge and the forward rocks
would break free and slide back toward me, not
down and forward out of the mouth, guaranteeing
one instant death! I immediately dubbed this "The
Cougar's Quickening Cave." I understand that much
of Buddhist contemplation is on the transitory
nature of all life and also on death. I see that this
cave would definitely enhance those musings!

I wondered with enough time in here, would that
imminence of death dwindle and the practice would
actually become boring? I doubt it after I realized the
top was only 15 feet away and there were trees on
top with roots slowly making their way into the cave,
opening up fresh water channels, etc.

I also wondered how long has this cave really been in existence since it isn't known very widely by anyone? There is no beaten path up here and it is next to impossible to approach from the left or the right.

Good thing daylight was waning which gave me only 10 minutes in the cave to contemplate life, my life, my excuse to leave it was thus not fear but time. Good thing I know well the last half hour back down the mountain in the dark. I am though, a little conflicted about the future time spent here. This is dangerous. I could develop the safe, false cave that is closer to Panther and much easier to get to, but as Hawkwind sings, "It is the nature of man to be dangerous."

Synchronicity: the day after I left Mount Shasta, I continued reading in the last chapter of Ian Bakers book, *The Heart of the World,* where he said some of their team heard enchanting singing down in the gorge while trying to sleep that last night.

One elder native later said, "We often hear such singing and we hear voices, but never see anyone and although we can hear the words we can't understand the meanings."

"Choeden told me that they often hear duets sung between a male and a female. Sometimes they hear voices calling their names, but there is never anyone to be seen."

"The singing comes as a blessing of Dorje Pagmo," Choeden asserted. "Your friends are lucky."

The Buddhist Tantras assert that Dakinis dwell equally in the outer phenomenal world as well as in the subtle energy channels of the adept's body. When duly acknowledged they sever the cords of thinking that constrain perception and open doors to realms of scintillating interdependence, beyond the boundaries of self-limiting desires. The dream songs of the Dakinis, half heard, half imagined, totally unverifiable, open us up to the innermost landscapes of the heart when we abandon efforts to edit experience and flow fearlessly into the mysterious heart of things.

Latrobe, PA.

by Mitch McCarrell

Once I thought nothing was a greater gift than the
next ride, some door opening into my life, call it
Ford, Chrysler, or Chevrolet.

Once a sad girl near Porterville, California, taking me
home to her favorite bar and is lets them see us
come in together. There were lessons to be learned
from her concern or their indifference. What was I
left each time to find?

Hitchhiking for heartaches, an old lover told me
once, bitter that I could leave so easily, just step out
by the highway, and buy into that dream: name a
Jack, Kerouac, or London, or all the way back to
bindlestiffs and bums, seeking some magic, the
mundane everyday life refused.

Always I started north and ended there: what use for
stories with no one to tell them to? Latrobe, PA,
five above, home to that great beer, as cold as it
would ever get, I thought, but then hitching for
Duluth, mid-Minnesota, midwinter, the bank
thermometer across the street, twelve below zero,
mid-day.

To think warm, I would turn south and redeye I-5, easy enough in day, palms waving like welcome wagons near Red Bluff, the air somewhat exotic, or all the way, Merida on the Yucatan, once, twice, and Key West at midnight one other. Back here again, it was parlor tricks for those who stayed behind, trucker talk, interstates, and homosexual come-ons near military bases. Coming home to friends and family who held faith inexorably with job and routine, trusting the supermarket not to move the bread aisle, making babies, and wondering how I could live without sureties.

But I had this: sooner or later somebody always stopped. Knowing that I would get where I was going finally, always, but that it wouldn't matter.

And it's only been here, lately, now in this later time where the road doesn't open endlessly out, I realize, I remember, almost too late, that it was the going, the going, and the going, and the going, that was good.

They would always ask what I learned. But I think now, "What was it I thought I had to learn?"

Entiat Valley

by Katharine Kiendl

Two weeks have come and gone and for two weeks I have been working for the Forest Service. Talks of fires are rampant with each day, fresh muscle and calloused hands enthusiastically dog to work. I stand back in awe, wondering how I came to all this.

Wildland firefighting, known to most East Coast city dwellers (of which I do derive) only through brief segments on the news, is my new profession. My office? The woods, no, not the woods, burning forests of flame and snag, of ash and root, ember and rock. My new home. Sixteen-hour days. Seven days a week. In dry, hot conditions. Under exhaustion, dehydration, and fatigue. It is death, life and laughter and every moment in-between. And this season I have made it mine. Where do these choices conspire? How do these desires persist?

It's hard to say what possessed me. There is my upbringing. A northern Virginia suburb of D.C., home of liberal progressives, well-funded education systems, government employees, and contractors galore. Metro rides reflect the power and networks that reside there, a sea of button downs and khakis, of heels and loafers, crowd each metro car. I stand there now, grown, down jacket stained, and duct taped, boots worn and two years too old. I used to ride this rail to meet my friends and now this routine once so familiar is alien and unbecoming (unfaithful to the woods I know).

To know what is wrong though is better than knowing nothing at all. Dazed, I spent one summer at home, feeling some sort of angst around each corner. Job shadows and feigned networking enforced this dread. I realized that home was no longer home and would never be again. But I wasn't just leaving home. I was leaving everyone I knew.

My friends from college had all pooled within the nearby city limits. How easy it would be to just step back in place, to be just as young and confused as we were in school. I loved them, I love them, I will cherish them until I lay, but being with them reminded me of how lost I felt. They are the strongest women you will meet, to not know your will amongst them will make you shrink if you haven't learned how to stand already. I yearned to be near mountains, I didn't enjoy the nights out on the city. No, no it wasn't for me.

The path was slow, switch backing up gentle grades. I followed my dreams, allowing them to draw my map. Once I saw myself driving across a long bridge, across water and speckled humps of land. Some were bare, filled with yellowed grasses, others were blue resembling arctic lain ice. Sky was heavy, pregnant with rain, water turquoise, deepest and purest of its kind. In other dreams I saw conifers lining coastlines clinging like velvet to every piece of ground. Wind swept through clouds combing through treetops and I floated on, looking down on it all. Breathing it in, watching the hydrology respire, cooling, collecting, rising, and turning down once again.

I had been to the Northwest once before I moved out here as a student biking across the Olympic Peninsula. Determined for no reason at sixteen to join the annual school bike trip. In mirrors I saw a beast; eyes misshapen, jowls from head to neck, body warped and distorted. Body became prison, and I desired not for strength or grit, but for shine and luster. Nights existed where I wished for the ability to purge, when I desired the will to resist food, and wished and hoped I could go a day without eating so that a pound could be shed. I tried and luckily in this I failed. Prior to that trip, I had prayed for an eating disorder. I had taken sharp edges to my skin, I had binged on Diet Cokes, and Slim Jims, and Twix bars, and everything unhealthy you can imagine. I was sure I was nothing to no one. And then this trip came. At first a whimsical glance of suggestion that somehow settled into steely determination. Where do these choices conspire? How do these desires persist?

I trailed the pack in the beginning, miles behind, near tears after walking up the first hill. I dreaded each day. Each minute I pedaled felt like an eternity and then somehow in some way it began to change. I convinced myself I could continue, sweeping my legs forward for just a minute more, and then five, and then ten, and then lost I became in the hours thereafter. After three weeks of heavy riding, of lugging 30 lbs. of food and gear, I began to desire the hum of my tires. I began to love the blurred concentration of asphalt, scoping in and out constantly. The line in front always sharp, everything around it hazed into black oblivion. There is no thinking in existing, no hate in just a moment.

After this trip, I understood my body in a new way. I took pride in its strength and tried desperately to shake off any self-doubt I already had. But while one moment can feel transformative and certainly be so, it's one building block towards the end result. You must learn to suspend and stretch that moment over time, and that work must be constant and without shame (there is no failure in continuing the work, does a tree not always grow?). While that experience was a step towards who I am today, it would be years, ten in fact (this is the tenth) until that journey finally ended on solid footing; in a body strong with the value of its worth. And while this journey has been in many ways slow going, I have arrived exactly on time. No moment in any other way would have solidified this foundation.

Many people, who have suffered from depression or anxiety, will tell you some oddly hopeful things (or perhaps hope is the wrong word, *Abandon It,* as Pemma Chodron once said). That even though many days can feel like an endless struggle, that even though often they live for others outside themselves, their torment, that pain gives them greater joy than they would know otherwise. It is only at night you see the stars (words echoed in forum on forum on forum), that holding such sadness in one's heart ultimately opens the eye to simple joy, to the beauty of a mindful act, that the wind brushing over the trees can replenish any soul (at least it does mine).

I am grateful for this thing I have inside of me. That while it digs in some way it rotates my clock hands forward still. And regardless of what it does, I am here, peace is my choice. A conscious action I seek every day.

This dread I know has other benefits. I am beginning to see it bloom in full, discovering each aspect. When you've felt sadness stagnant in your belly, no present action can overwhelm.

At work we hike, we are told we have it easy, we move straight up screed valley walls (*steeper than a cow's face*), blowing through brush and perhaps soon ash. *The weak ones make us stronger,* they say, *push yourself to the limit,* they demand, *don't stop, just don't ever stop,* they whisper. We practice hiking in a line, shuffling messages back and forth, words tripping over exhausted breath, annunciation poorer than piss. *Repeat? Copy? Clear?* Where did the message get dropped? Who is not being accountable? Who is not giving their all?

I trail behind again like I did ten years before sucking in air, feeling my heart give, and take, and thump, and thwack. Labored, I breathe heavy. I follow each step telling myself only five minutes more (more, and more, and more). I am slow, a rookie, new to the fold. They don't know what's inside. That each labored breath is one I am grateful for, that every time my thigh burns and I move further up these seemingly endless canyon walls, I am still somehow at peace. They see me red faced, dirt crusted lips, eyebrows in upwards crescent moons, and they see confusion, concern, fear, or so it seems. You see, when you are a woman and you do anything but smile, the assumption is a struggle lies where a smile should be cemented still.

Gathered at the top of a hike this past week, a crew lead took us into a circle. Sharp blue eyes, blond, and ginger bearded, he looked at all of us like a hawk sizing it's ground and standing next to me began to speak.

Firefighting is not for everyone.

Deep breath, pause.

Some of you aren't cut out for this.
I am not trying to be a dick, but if this is hard for you,
then you shouldn't be here.

Breathe catches, muffled in throat.

Your team is depending on you.
DO NOT
let your team down.

Words spitting like fire spotting down a canyon, stinging my unbroken skin, his voice right next to mine, his words echoing into my ears, the self-doubt attempting invasion.

What they don't know is that I am stronger than

them. Yes those hotshots and rappellers with 50 pounds of muscle on me. *I am stronger than you, I will not stop,* I say silently. They see my face exhausted, red, breath in tow, and catching itself in circles. They think I will be quick to fold.

But I have already been broken and I have made myself again. No hike will return me to the child I was. I stand next to him, unsure of what to do, do I smile defiantly? Do I stay straight-faced staring into oblivion? Do I pull him aside and tell him he's wrong? That I am tougher than I look? No. S*how don't tell,* do *more with less* and *don't stop moving* they whisper, *don't stop moving.*

It Goes Like This

by Gloria Piper Roberson

Her way is like a button on a tatty sweater: there, yet quiet.

It goes like this—I see the door ajar two doors down from my apartment. Emmy Rathbone lives there. I don't know her personally only that she is timeworn, lives alone, uses a white cane, does her own shopping at nearby Grover's around the corner at the end of Grover Street. I know this because I shop there, too. Seth, the box boy, helps Emmy fill her shopping list, walks her back, and then shelves her groceries. Seth tells me this.

We occasionally pass in our hallway. I know she knows I am there, yet she swings her cane and walks right by without a word, or a nod. Each time when I say *Hello, Ms. Rathbone* I sense that she likes it— likes hearing her name, likes that someone knows it, that someone calls it out. Yet, she toddles on, swinging her cane like turning pages in a seed catalog, looking for something special to plant in the spring.

I push the door open a little and then step in calling her name. Our apartments are matching sets. The difference is Emmy's is orderly like food on a plate that never touches. Mine is mulligan stew.

I peek in her bedroom. It goes like this—tutus in every color, size, and style masks the walls with as many toe shoes, and tiaras—jeweled, feathered, silver and gold. Waterless vases hold dusty, dried bouquets; petal slivers clutter the floor. All over the room sits framed photographs of a ballerina leaping, spinning, and on tiptoes with arms high, hands drooping over her head like daffodils. Mounted programs sit on anything that is flat, including the floor, publicizing Emmy Rathbone's performances in France, and Germany, Russia, Australia, Canada, and the United States—the steamer trunk at the foot of the bed tattooed with decals proves it. The room is a shrine without candles.

I check in the kitchen and then I knock on the bathroom door. I again risk a glance. I find her embraced in bubbles. Her head resting in the curve of the porcelain tub, her eyes closed, peacefully soaking. Wilted, lifeless breasts tell me different. I call 911. Then it goes like this—I sit by the tub. I wait. I wait for the police, the ambulance, and then the coroner. I answer questions.

Are we related? A police officer asks.

No. I say.

Did we talk much?

Never. I did try. She was like an untold secret.

Does she have family? The officer asks.

I don't know. I say.

How long did she live here?

I don't know. She lived here when I moved in twelve
years ago.

The coroner rolls Emmy out of her apartment,
covered, on a gurney. He sees me, half smiles, and
says natural causes.

I stay in the bedroom a moment longer amongst a
time I never knew, and a time when a ballerina's
worn-out heart no longer must pretend. I believe
Emmy Rathbone danced her last performance in that
bubbly water had a standing ovation and flowers at
her feet. Her name echoed off the walls.

I step out into the hallway and close the door behind
me.

Chem Bank

by Mitch McCarrell

My friend says to me that Chemical Bank of New
York is not a good group to mess with.

"Connections," he says. He tells me this, months
after I've accepted their generous offer—a gold credit
card and a $7000 credit line.

"It's your lifeline," he says, "you need worry about."

He can be hard to read, peculiar in humor, and
messing with people's minds.

Connected. In one shattering, less-than serendipitous
moment he destroys months of loving rumination
over the strangeness of their name, that quirky
juxtaposition, "Chemical Bank of New York,"
as if in some huge molecular mistake, chemists and
financiers had suddenly merged—perhaps a full
rupturing and bungled reassembly of the time-space
continuum, clouds boiling in primordial wonder.
Sometimes chaos can call forth chaos, no theory.

Chem Bank was all of that to me and more—men in
white lab coats, piles of cash like those in Scrooge
McDuck's vault, erlenmeyer flasks, bunsen burners,
petri dishes, capillary viscometers, pinchcocks,

penetrometers (science can be so goddamned erotic), all set in the Empire State, boat rides on the Hudson, Manhattan at the turn of the century, knickerbocker society, and high greed: Asters, Vanderbilts, Van Renassaellers. Or take that other funny Dutch name, Schuyler, a name that any culturally impoverished westerner like myself, short on spelling choices for stopped dental plosives, would spell simply with a "k" and no "u."

All that sweet bemusal wiped out in one ugly image. *Connected.* I think my friend means mob and I wonder if he means that seriously. I run through what I know for sure about him.

A friendship of three years goes by in a split second: all lives should pass so quickly. Fellow inmates of a plumbing and electric supply house, briefly, we were confused as relatives to the point where I began introducing him as my illegitimate son.

His wife had run off with his brother-in-law: oddly enough those two had been related only by marriage. Later she settled down with a guy from back east who'd done time—second-degree murder: just in the wrong place at the wrong time, the new hubby said. But I digress.

Bankrupt. How could this happen to me? Self-pity, sure, but not my only shortcoming. I, who for a lifetime, had been too smart to buy on credit—a peasant's failing, trusting only so far out ahead, never buying anything advertised on TV, not even golden oldies so pure that only dead men could have created them. For me, used cars only. Clothes in the off-season, sweaters in June, swimming trunks at tax time, marked-down meat only slightly brown, where the chemicals were failing.

How could I sign away money I would never have? In truth, only partly in a moment of weakness, half-crazed by divorce and my ex-wife walking away with a big check and me standing there saying "wah, wah, wah; this isn't fair." In divorce the wise take their licking and move on.

But no. Cleanly gleaned and plucked, I sought to return the favor, only the ex was invincible, and even worse, gone. And then one day, there in the mailbox, the letter from Chem Bank, their generous offer. I thought them naïve. Trusting.

Or maybe, in a moment of something like insanity, I thought I had been handed the sword, you know the one, and the world, "reality", for lack of a better word, demanded I teach those silly bankers a lesson they surely needed to learn.

And now it comes to this. They want their money back. My friend, he keeps saying they are one bad "they."

I appeal to him, his reputation as a bit of a shithouse lawyer, a man who's had his day in court, wrote his own divorce papers, bankrupted on his wife's shopping debts, a piece of bad luck driving (a corvette in an intersection—$60,000 in the blink of an eye), a man who stared justice in the eye, and pleaded for clearer insured driver laws. Why not use his expertize, I think. "Lay it out for me man," I say. "What are my options, what's the best way to proceed?"

And so, he explains bankruptcy court pleadings, trustees, filing dates, mean cross-examinations.

And then he brings up the other again: I've picked a bad bunch to mess with. They may not resort to normal measures in attempting to recover their investment. The mob. And this in my life just as I had become so sure that there was nothing worse than an ex-wife. Perhaps, he says thoughtfully, this might be an opportunity to get taken into the Federal Witness Protection Program, where I would learn to live by certain key phrases: "Don't look at me; you don't know me, keep walking."

Who could believe salvation so simple as a sleepover at Janet Reno's house?

In the new life FBI agents will give me, I will wake one day in my bed to find that I am thirty-two again, or thirty-four, but not more than thirty-five at the most.

On my first walk out into that sunlit world, I'll encounter the woman who had been my wife. A woman overwhelmed by her biological clock and struck balancing the population race in favor of English speaking northern European bloodstock. "Keep walking," I'll tell her. "Keep walking."

And yes, my hair will be back, in aces, all of it, every goddamned little strand, dark and heavy there on the front of my head like some cock's plume, radiant and waving in the breeze, too good to be believed.

On a weekday afternoon, I'll play basketball for hours, too irresponsible and in my prime to quit until I've sweated my jockstrap full.

And I'll get roaring drunk on government money, obnoxious, loud, knee-crawling, accursed of bartenders, hump the hostess, down and dirty drunk, and I'll wake the next morning feeling like a

god, trusting fully in life, with it all out there before
me, alive to possibility and knowing that poets will
sing my story, in beautifully rhymed, perfectly metric
heroic couplets, positive, glowing, patriotic hopeful
poetry, praising life and asking God for not one
fucking thing more.

And did I tell you? This friend of mine, he's Church
of Christ, although I've yet to see him in that context.
A world where light falls effortlessly, endlessly, away
from darkness, each spilling off into its own domain,
as it should.

And what better salvation could the righteous or
unrighteous of either sex desire, than a world such
as that, where all assume the innocence of children
and are forgiven their sins, without fear of ligation.

Déjà Vu (Original)

by Claudia Yvette Zamorano

En ocasiones sueño que mueres. Miento. Solo lo hice la otra noche después de que quisiste matarte. Quisiera decirte que, al enterarme, quise llenarme de lágrimas, gritar con el sentir de una actuación de telenovelas. Pero no. No fue así.

Lo cierto es que me vi sentada, pensando en el viaje de carretera que nunca hicimos, los óleos que nos quedaron pendientes, en la vida en la cual ya no podríamos encontrarnos.

Quise morirme, pero en cambio tan solo desperté para segundos a después volver a dormir. Recobrar el conocimiento fue mi manera de escapar, suicidarme de un sueño. Volví a dormir y no sé qué pasó, pero, al despertar, quería que estuvieses conmigo, borracho o con resaca y una pachita de alcohol, la cual podríamos mezclar en nuestros cafés, caminar, llorar, y reír de la estupidez de la noche anterior.

Digerí el desayuno primero que el sueño. El internet ahora es la escena llena de flashbacks, canciones tristes, y personas saliendo de sus casas caminando por la calle, viendo, escuchando cosas que les recuerdan a la persona amada.

Déjà Vu (Translation)

by Claudia Yvette Zamorano

Sometimes I dream that you die. I lie. I only did it the other night, after you wanted to kill yourself. I would like to tell you that, when I found out, I wanted to fill myself with tears, and scream in the mode of a TV novella performance. But no, it was not like that.

The truth is that I saw myself sitting, thinking about the road trip we never made, the paintings that were left unfinished, in this life in which we could no longer find each other anymore.

I wanted to die, but instead I only woke up for a few seconds, soon to return to sleep. Recovering my awareness was my way of escape, of committing suicide from a dream. I went back to sleep and I do not know what happened, but, when I woke up, I wanted you to be with me, drunk or with a hangover and a little bottle of alcohol, which we could mix into our coffees, walk, cry, and laugh at the stupidity of the previous night.

I digested breakfast before the dream. The internet is now the scene full of flashbacks, sad songs, and people walking out of their houses walking down the street, watching, listening to things that remind them of the loved one.

Así me sentí yo, pero sin salir de mi casa, sin bañarme, con mi café espresso rebajado con leche de coco y miel de abeja.

Los videos musicales de youtube me recordaban a ti y a nuestros malos chistes (más míos que tuyos). Miraba al baboso de Leon Laguerri y me acordaba de ti. Son tan parecidos. Miento. Pero sonríen igual de bonito, de la misma forma igual de egoísta porque los dos sonríen para ustedes mismos.

Veo culos, selfies en el espejo, y arte en Instagram de algunos artistas urbanos que seguro te encantarán; pero bueno, apenas simpatizas con Facebook y sus putos memes donde todos se burlan de ti, y de mí, y de todos. Te veo en Facebook, pero no planeo hablarte, estas fuera de línea.

Intento recordar que estas en el trabajo y no muerto en tu habitación; siempre es lo mismo revisar si hiciste alguna publicación, si tu novia habló de ti hoy en su muro, saber si tienes vida.

Ahora tienes 14 horas fuera de línea no sé dónde metido.

This is how I felt, but without leaving my house, without bathing, with my espresso coffee reduced with coconut milk and bee honey.

The YouTube music videos reminded me of you and our bad jokes (more mine than yours). I looked at Leon Laguerri's foolery and I remembered you. You two are so similar. I lie. But you both smile just as nicely, in the same way selfishly, because you both smile for yourselves.

I see asses, selfies in the mirror, and urban art on Instagram that you will surely love; but it's well if you only sympathize with Facebook and its fucking memes that all make fun of you, and me, and everyone. I see you on Facebook, but I do not plan on talking to you, you're offline.

I try to remember that you are at work and not dead in your room; it is always the same, checking to see if you made some publication, if your girlfriend talked about you today on her wall, to know if you are alive.

Now you have been offline for 14 hours, who knows where.

Me cuestiono si hoy estuviste en línea y por qué no me hablaste. Trato de tranquilizarme y recuerdo que ahora no tengo nada nuevo que contar. Quisiera decirte que esto solo fue una vez hace dos semanas, pero cada tercer día recuerdo que en cualquier momento puede ser tu ultima conexión y me asusto.

Me dan ganas de creer en dios, comprar una veladora, un rosario; recordar el credo, rezar el avemaría, arrodillarme durante horas, y pedir que tu vida se acabe después de la mía.

Que egoísta soy siempre queriendo que las vidas de mis seres amados se terminen después de la mía.

No quiero sufrir; yo no quiero saber si te estás matando del cansancio en el trabajo o te estás matando frente al espejo de tu habitación.

Espero volverte a regalar rosas antes de verme obligada a llevarte cempasúchil.

I ask myself if you were online today and wonder why you did not speak to me. I try to calm myself down and I remember that now I have nothing new to say. I would like to tell you that this was only once two weeks ago, but every third day I remember that at any moment it could be your last connection and I get scared.

It makes me want to believe in God, purchase a candle, a rosary; remember the Creed, recite Hail Mary's, kneel for hours, and ask that your life end after mine.

How selfish I am, always wanting the lives of my loved ones to end after mine.

I do not want to suffer; I do not want to know if you're killing yourself from fatigue at work or you're killing yourself in front of the mirror in your room.

I hope to give you roses again before I'm forced to bring you Marigolds...

Mirrored Self

by Jessica Mitchell

I wear your face like a mask

as I wander lost in the darkness

tripping over broken sagebrush

and choking on the smell of tears

I am lost to the wonders of starry nights

shielded through slit eye lids

marked black and blue with past transgressions

I am every heel stomped

heart pounding

blood drop dripped

from battered elbows

and torn knees

I am you in the mirror when you can't see yourself

I am friday nights and sunday morning

spent bent over a bowl or a pew

screaming my god till your throat aches

and bile drowns the taste of regrets

Tears Of A Masked Face

by Tyler Burlingame

I am the sickness of my own heart. A crestfallen
example of a breaking heart, and in bitter reality, am
a member of an old tedious dancing bear collecting
circus troupe. To jest and form balloons is my steady
task yet one was not given to me, nay for no one did I
ask. For I have been the head of this crazy group of
modern day gutter rats and call us a mafia if you
may, but we're to be held down by no man. And I, a
clown, sit in a solemn way around and face the
corner and am different indeed; I shed these paint
mixed tears and let my sorrows drown, I do not lie
nor intend to mislead.

Born in the mountains long ago, I was raised to be
violent, and accept what comes from great sorrow,
and that I may better understand life if I face death.
Whoever would stand in my way or attempt to
dissuade, they would surely be cut down and ever
since I've been claiming my turfs in different towns.

We travel as a circus, but with precise malice do we
infect; the mentally unstable and the children
parents chose to neglect. We take them, as they are,
to become travelers of afar. The fate held in store for
the increasingly more and more can only be to my

hope and plea, to capture as many forsaken souls as the devil will allow me.

We come with laughter, and fun, and quite good will, but after some time, the ink will dry on the end of your creative quill. Then what is to be? You fall in my larcenous arms, lazy and discontent. I am the sickness of your heart and these sins do I lament.

Can't you comprehend my quite clear confession? I am the spider's den, the secrets of gossip never heard therein, yet hold such immense power over imagination. I am the hatred of your heart and I've been given the power to tear you apart. I dwell in the depths yet also in your cup of tea. I am always there and will smite if you let me. Many choose to deny what they might see, but evil's within you as well as the good is in me. The hurricane has been twisting around our heads most atrociously since Zion wasn't history. I am coming clean to help you understand because to every woe there is a man.

Now that I've told you what makes up the majority of me, you can marvel at yourself in awesome joviality. Spread the word, I plea, for it is the future if we cannot spread more disasters presently.

Because I am a conduit of evil, I hold the righteousness within me. We all hope for the utopian eternity, regardless of our previous childhood catastrophes. I try to make it most dramatic like a soap opera writer, and that you won't notice my evil, and the true form of myself; a clownish, crying spider.

Steel-Barbed Words

by L. Burton Brender

lord - you search the
heart as no man can

you look deeply into the
places no one can see

how frightening
that is to me

I tremble at the thought
of my wickedness laid bare

to others I play the arrogance of
my heart off as a joke

I pretend my steel-barbed words
are horseplay

I convince myself
that this is true

twice - three times I
lie to my own conscience
but you know the truth
of my heart - oh lord

you see the pride I flatter
myself with

your spirit convicts
me of my sin

it crushes my pride like
a millstone

forgive me my well-hidden hatreds
that I may forsake them

see my iniquities just once
that I may learn from my transgressions

have mercy on my soul
oh lord

grant your servant the grace
that he does not deserve

The Good Ship Jesus

by Heather Kristoffersen

(Launched October -1562)

a pen
frozen white
with oil ink
falling towards the doiled table

the crystal glasses hold their breath

fractures
split across the porcelain
every buck of the pen
springs a new web of oil
across the once unblemished
surface

the black is screaming
on top of the cool table
like blood soaked snow
loud enough
that even the determined ear cannot ignore
no glances at what's left
of the unadulterated white
can be stolen away
from the reaching fingers
of the black as rich as crimson

bleeding out

the oil melts the ice
with fleeting heat
and dances
with the flowing white

VII

Dreamers

by Anabel Watson

I dreamed of an unknown dimension
that nobody reaches
but those who can see
the patterns aboard a carpet of water
they tread on its surface quite effortlessly

and when they have tread on this palace of oceans
they spot in the distance
an isle of blue sapphire stone
and the intrinsic flavor of notions
tells them they journeyed to land at their home

so looking across this blue dappled sea
glazed in a moonlight
and full of a soft frisky air
they set foot on this island
appealing to those in a world so far but yet near

sometimes a whisper
a haunting that enters my mind
will allure me with wisps of an image that rides
on the currents invitingly calling
to learn and to try to become what they hide

the feeling is lost so maybe I'm not
one who can grasp the whole pattern

to enter that world

but I hope that those who are dreamers

will find for themselves this world that's their own

perchance are you a dreamer?

Step One
by Adam Leonardini

take your upper lip
and attach it to your neck
feel the wind on your teeth

floating ribs
have meaning
when crucifixion
takes place

is time that of stonehenge?
or that of an inhale?
do you have
the contextual attachment to time?
who owns it?
where does it come?
stop stop stop

go

aging faces peer in shock
at the lie of context

who are you?
the picture heeds

aged hands no longer able to hold
the descendants

there is only a singular time

tick tock
motherfucker

Proof Is For Those Who Need Belief

by Matthew Genther

I saw a man hold back a caravan of war machines in
the middle of the road with his arms at his side, a
bag of survival in each hand, but I can't prove it.

Nothing's bad, but nothing's real. I saw a monk in
full lotus. He sunk into his own mind, dumped his
body outside and put it on fire till everyone on-
looking saw him burn black and fall away, but I can't
prove it in this hologram where nothing's bad, but
nothing's real.

I saw the hologram of a hologram of a Boeing 767,
flight 11 hit the north tower on September 11th
synchronized almost perfectly with the C.I.A. thumb
that detonated that shit to the ground, but I'll never
prove it, not in this yellow half of a green hologram
where nothing is bad, because nothing's real.

But she's on her way back—baby blue. I saw my
subtle body turned out in the eyes of another's body,
and she said she'd stay with me through and
through as we traversed the ether between worlds as
queen and king of the universe. She said, "you go
first," and I did, and she followed, and when we
touched back down I couldn't prove it without the
other half of a green hologram where nothing's bad,

185

but nothing's real, but she's on her way back around—our long lost baby blue sister star.

I saw the green body of Osiris diced up into thirteen pieces, a price upon his offspring Horus and Jesus, and then the snake with his tail stole her away and left a constellatory trail in my memory, but I can't prove it, because "I saw" backwards spells "Was I?"

She's been gone so long I can't remember. If I don't know why I'm living in a fake world, what the fuck am I gonna do when it gets real in this hologram where nothing's bad, but nobody feels!?

I ask others in this world, but they can't remember either. They think I'm blonde with green eyes. They think I'm called Matthew. They name everything cause they can't remember who made it. They think they know who my mother is! I met a luminous angel with orange fuzzy skin, she looked like an electric peach, and she told me that her mother-ship has better schools than my time-ship Earth. She told me that reality occurs after two cone-shaped spirals turn in on each other and connect in the center of an omni-directional holographic cube who likes to think of itself as a sphere.

She said, "Stop time traveling. You're already home," and I said, "Prove it," and she didn't. Proof is for those who need belief, and this is a hologram where nothing's bad, but nothing's real.

Untitled

by Christine Ingram

I've dug a grave for myself
it is too narrow to lie
I sit up

---

commitment to a commitment
"I've seen it all" she says
and continues to live in a box
where all there's to be seen
are muddy walls

---

a despair so parasitic
one could only dream of moving forward
(but)
decidedly never will

Thoughts Murmured Prior To A Blackout And Shouted After A Moment Of Clarity

by Michael Reed Schooler

these are broken things
sounding out broken notes
which fly with broken wings
out of my broken throat
and these are broken strings
upon this broken boat
and from these broken dreams
alone I have to float

Cecilia

by Jessica Mitchell

I exist on the edge

in the in between before night swallows the blue sky

I exist in the blues and purples

in the sea spray salty mist in my hair

one day I will rise past the setting sun

until then I only have this moment

each night

before the tears streak sand across my face

and I dare not wipe them away

Upon Seeing Mars

by Kevin Strickland

the heavens are never more vivid

than when shining on a dark place

and they leave nothing to speak of majesty

yet in their magnificence they are

only what they are

other worlds

other stars

still

one can't help but wonder

what magic they may hold

or beings who upon seeing

reflect and feel cold

Stop And Smell The Plastic Roses

by Mike Morgan

I've discovered a place where time stands still

a magical place for sure

as if I'm invisible

everything stops

eternity frozen and pure

I meditate

and I focus my thoughts

and I cannot for sure tell you how

but all of my worries start melting away

letting me focus on now

It's not hard to find it if you want to try

this magical secret of mine

just go to your nearest walmart store

and get in the checkout line

Instrucciones para Fumar (Original)

by Claudia Yvette Zamorano

Primero que nada, usted debe contar con un valle de muerte, envolverlo en un papel o bien ponerlo en una pipa. Recuerde antes sacar todos esos peces que están de más. Sujete este mar y colóquelo entre sus labios, tome el encendedor, cerillos o cualquier artefacto que contenga fuego, una vela quizás.

Comience a inhalar, mientras el fuego comience a incendiarlo todo. Ahora usted y la lumbre deben hacer mancuerna y consumir juntos el agua salada, pero esto conlleva traición. El fuego no destruirá nada; usted consumirá el fuego y al mar. Una vez que haya comenzado a consumir a estos dos, llegando el humo, usted deberá fluir con él, después, al extinguir este mar, usted irá sintiendo relajación y extrema libertad.

Instructions For Smoking (Translation)

by Claudia Yvette Zamorano

Before anything, you must have a valley of death, wrap it in a paper or put it in a pipe. Remember to first remove all fish that are in the way. Hold this sea and place it between your lips, take the lighter, matches or any device that contains fire, a candle perhaps.

Begin inhalation, while the fire starts to burn everything. Now you and the fire must work together and jointly consume the salt water, but this involves betrayal. The fire will not destroy anything; you will consume the fire and the sea. Once you have begun to consume these two, the smoke having arrived, you should flow with it, and while extinguishing this sea, you will feel relaxation and extreme freedom.

Swallow

by Kevin Strickland

time and fate mix pleasantries
they laugh as peasants fair
they toast to age and tragedy
agreeing neither cares

from golden goblets spills a blood-red wine
lines of tombstones boast their wares
despite the drunks we peasants love
and live what life we're spared

since infinity grew from a quickening
out of nothingness with what exists
mother nature has infused her brood
in stars she strewed wild on a black abyss

now theories of everything exist
but only one with relativity to me
on how the whole blasted catastrophe occurred
so that I may know my loved ones kiss
and belong like a moon to the earth he can't resist

and so emphatically I insist
let fate ground and devour our mortality
and in times belly may I sour and swell
but know before they fill my hole
I've had their finest merlot

and as for the crumbs of soul that I stole
I swallowed

Rojo Cereza (Original)

by Ulises Navarro

Estaba corriendo en medio de los cerezos tratando de salir de ahí, corrí entre cientos y cientos de árboles.

Cerezas en el suelo y hojas por montones, era de día, pero se veía tan oscuro, cuando ya no supe a donde dirigirme, sin ver una luz de referencia para salir de ese campo de grandes y frondosos árboles, me sentí atrapado y la música, las voces todo desapareció, en ese instante como si me hubiese transportado, a otro sitio y solo me encontraba ahí, me detuve y observé con ese miedo infantil de no saber que sucedía.

¿Acaso todos se habían ido?

Vi algo, como un venado moverse por uno de los pasillos de árboles y mi cuerpo se congeló, quedé inmóvil, caminé hacia un gran árbol y decidí esconderme detrás de él, empezaba todo a verse más tenue y lúgubre, solo un poco luz que entraba de entre las copas de los árboles, decidí tomar un camino y corrí, corrí y corrí, como en las pesadillas cuando huyes y no llegas a ningún lado; quise brincar, quise gritar, pero mi voz se escondió.

Cherry Red (Translation)

by Ulises Navarro

I was running through the cherry trees, trying to escape; I wove between hundreds and hundreds of trees.

Cherries on the ground and leaves everywhere. It was daytime, but the sky was so dark. When I could no longer orient myself, without the locus of any light to guide me out of that orchard of large leafy trees, I felt trapped, and the music, the voices, everything disappeared. In that instant, as if transported to another place where I was alone, I stopped. And I observed with that childlike fear of not knowing what was happening.

Had everybody left?

I saw something, like a deer moving along a row of the trees, and my body froze. I was immobile. I walked toward a large tree and decided to hide behind it. Everything was becoming dim and dreary, only a bit of light filtering through the treetops. I started down a pathway and I ran. I ran and ran, like in those nightmares where you trying to escape and don't arrive anywhere at all. I wanted to jump. I wanted to shout. But my voice hid.

Yo no sé, pero me enmudecí, seguí corriendo, cuando tropecé con una raíz de un árbol viejo ya caído, asustado, en la sombra, tan pequeño e inofensivo, de cara al suelo no sabía, pero estaba huyendo, no supe porque o de qué, pero mi ropa manchada de rojo por la cereza en el suelo que aplasté al caer; ¡me levanté otra vez y me di cuenta que podría ser un sueño!, así que me abofeteé la cara pero el dolor era real. Me subí a un árbol y decidí buscar en lo alto la salida, pero no había tal, eran filas y filas interminables de árboles, la agujeta de mi bota se atoró en un pequeño alambre y me hizo caer desde lo alto del árbol, sentí tanto miedo mientras caía; no tenía salida, estaba solo y tal vez moriría por la altura, así que si la caída me mataba tal vez podría salir de esa horrible sensación y dejaría de preocuparme por estar sin salida y solo.

Caí y al abrir mis ojos había cientos de personas rodeándome para auxiliarme, no me expliqué lo que pasó, no había árboles, no había cerezas, solo yo bañado en un gran charco de sangre debajo de ese gran puente.

And... I don't know... but I became mute. I kept running when I tripped on the root of an old fallen tree, scared in the shadows, so small and harmless with my face on the ground. I didn't know... but I was running, from what and for what cause I did not know. But my clothing was stained red from the cherries I squashed upon falling. I stood up and realized that this could all be a dream! So, I slapped myself, but the pain was real. I climbed a tree and decided to search for the exit from above. But such an exit didn't exist, only rows upon rows of endless trees. The shoelace of my boot caught on a small wire and I fell from way up in the tree. I felt such fear while I fell - I had no escape - I was alone, and perhaps I might die from the height. So [at least] if I died from the fall, I might perhaps escape that horrible sensation, I would stop worrying about being alone and without a way out.

I fell, and upon opening my eyes, there were hundreds of people gathering to help me. I couldn't explain what had happened. There were no trees, no cherries, just me, bathed in a puddle of blood under that big bridge.

Lost In The Night

by Sylvia B.

something's got the best of me

where's the rest of me

sometimes I forget how to breathe

hello 3 a.m.

I see the static

I feel the waves

stupid infomercials

I see my friends come around the corner

black eyes

I know they aren't real

or maybe I don't

I missed you

I couldn't sleep

I'm glad you joined me

Spiders As Friends

by Adam Leonardini

eyelids sewn to temples

passing through
impeded atmosphere
the wake of form
echoes of ancient void

seductive

primordial

mutters

transitory will falls prey
to scrutiny

autum-vitae transmutation
sustenance
piquancy of toil
preferred decadence
empathy
the understood lure

Blue Love

by Matthew Genther

There is an abysmal voice in my head these days,
every day, all day verbalizing a spell memorized over
the beginning of an addicted adulthood.

The mechanisms of coping with the death of my
mother have pressed out a character, a thought-form
with vocal cords, the same cords that plug into the
pineal gland in the center of my head, the place
where "me" is, the location to which "I" refers. I close
my eyes to investigate the intruder.

He just looks like deep blackness like a lake in the
middle of the night. Where once I saw a soft Blue
crystal beneath the ripples of the veil, now I see
blackness. A mirror in the dark reflects nothing but
my feeling fingertips and maybe my forehead as I
lean into this other me and listen to his babbling
between my ears. From inane to insane, his vapid
voice is easily stimulated but not in the least bit
stimulating, so I breathe.

He slows down. I take another even deeper and a
third—the deepest. He shuts up. Carbon dioxide is
his food, fear is the marinade, acidity his habitat,
cancer his cousin the murderous fuck, but oxygen
seems to change him. I keep breathing, more in than

out, and the crystal hums a bit discordant at first, flat. Screaming turns to singing, and light shines on the mirror. Movement is life. This movement of light reminds me of my mother.

If we both Love the water, and that water is a river moving, then we have no choice but to agree on where the water goes and go with it together.

The voice doesn't sound disagreeable anymore.

Made in the USA
Middletown, DE
02 March 2019